Options Trading Beginners

A Step-By-Step Crash Course To Make Money and Create a Passive Income by Options Trading

Mattew Von Der Lyer

TABLE OF CONTENTS

CONSIDER THESE FIRST PRINCIPLES

- What are stocks?
- Before you take that first step
- Conventional approach to investing in stock?

THE SECRET SAUCE TO INVESTMENTS

- What is investment?
- Venture and Monetary Development Why do you need to invest?
- Motivations to enable you to put away your cash
- Types of investment

OPTION TRADING - A KEY TO SUCCESS

- What is an Option?
- A Fundamental Difference
- Key Takeaways
- Types of Option
- How Accomplish Option Works

HOW TO TRADE WITH THE TREND

- Buying Options Versus Selling Options
- Purchasing Calls and Puts
- Call Options: Buying Versus Selling
- Put Options: Buying Versus Selling

- Illustration of a short put vertical

- Trading checklist and Trading Plan: a dichotomy
- Importance of Trading Checklist

STEPWISE ACTION FOR SUCCESSFUL TRADE-IN OPTIONS TRADING

- Step-by-Step Action to Prepare for Trade
- Steps to Help You during a Trade Action

MAKING A TRADE

- Avoiding the pitfalls while you trade

SAVVY STEPS FOR SELECTING WINNERS

- VALUATION
- GROWTH
- PROFITABILITY

DIVERSIFICATION STRATEGIES

- Types of Diversification Strategy
- Diversify. Yes or No?
- Disadvantages Advantages

HOW TO CREATE A SUSTAINABLE PORTFOLIO

- How is a portfolio managed?
- Exchange-Traded Funds (ETFs)

INTRODUCTION

"An investment in knowledge pays the best interest."

Benjamin Franklin

Every human contest is controlled by those who possess matchless traits, skills, and capabilities required in their fields. The stock market is not left out. The various methods of investing among successful stock market players may differ from one person to another. However, to successfully trade in stocks, you must be acquainted with specific rules. A drift away from these essential qualities may take you down a path of regrets. Trust me, these qualities do not have to be inborn, but they can learnt and engaged with. This is why I've written this book; to bring the world of stock market to you.

Do you have fears for investing in stock? Are you disturbed that you may lose a large sum of your money if you take part in the stock market? Have you been told that stock investing is like gambling? The good news is that I'm glad that you've laid your hands on this book where you will learn, UN-learn, and re-learn everything you need to know about option trading and the stock market.

I like to say that investing in stock is not gambling. But the stock market is about investing in your resources and trading to achieve success.

In stock investing, your first valuable currency is to develop the right kind of mindset and emotional fit that will help you win big in the stock market. This should go side by side with the tactics and strategies you are learning. You must have these three essential keys; have a winning strategy, be determined to succeed, and always set your gaze at the optimistic side of life.

As a matter of fact, the landscape of investment profile can be tremendously dynamic and transitional. But anyone who makes out time to accurately fathom and understand the underlying philosophies and various assets stands to gain considerably over the long haul.

Stock Investing may be an overwhelming prospect for beginners, with a gross variety of conceivable assets to include in their portfolio. But this will always turn out well when the strategies are carefully and adequately engaged.

One of America's most successful stock trader, Mark Minervini, once said that "There's a difference between making a decent return in the stock market and achieving super performance, and this can be life- changing."

He added in a statement that it doesn't matter your position (Lawyer, Engineer, doctor, teacher, stay-at-home mom) in the spectrum of life; everyone can achieve super performance.

Therefore, in the pages of this book, you'll learn timeless truth and expertise that will launch and position you for success in the stock market world. Get set because knowledge is the new gold.

This book is a guide to how you can trade Options for a Living and generate passive income with the Latest Proven Stock Market Strategies.

Get ready to

Know and distinguish between the three types of investments Know the types of risks involved in investing

Be acquainted with the strategy of the iron condor Understand option trading probabilities

Build confidence in your investments plan and adjust your portfolio to help you make bigger bets.

CHAPTER ONE

CONSIDER THESE FIRST PRINCIPLES

"No wise pilot, no matter how great his talent and experience, fails to use his checklist."

– Charlie Munger

In the stock market, anybody can learn how to make money, but the secret to successfully invest in stock requires an exhaustive study of facts and principles of various strategies that are needed for trade.

Therefore, in this chapter, we'll condense some major investing principles that will give you a head start on understanding the winning philosophy. And so, let's explore some basic facts.

Explore the basics

Stock trading became an extremely successful enterprise during the late 1990s. Right from this time, it was seen that tennis stars and underground rockers got into the new market. Likewise, Financial specialists watched their stock portfolios, and stock-shared supports soar with the arrival and pre-eminence of the stock trading party, which formed what was seen as the last part of an 18-year rise (as buyers say) in stocks.

Interestingly, the United States venture movement became an incredible case for the immense popularity which the stock trading industry experienced during that time span. By 1999, a huge percentage of U.S. family units had become actively involved in the stock exchange market, turning the already popular venture into a literal household name.

However, millions lost their cash when there was a significant fall in the stock exchange market during 2000–2002. By the time of the fall, a huge number of individuals had also invested in the stock market, even though it appeared they did not quite understand, well enough, what they were putting their resources into. This could have been avoided if they had a simple comprehension of what stock truly was,

perhaps this could have brought about a strategic distance from some costly missteps.

The focus of this book is not just to inform you regarding the nuts and bolts of stock investing, but to also provide an insight into some methodologies and best practices that can help you draw maximum benefits from the stock exchange market. Before you contribute your first dollar, you have to comprehend the rudiments of stock contributing.

What are stocks?

Stocks are a value speculation asset range, akin to part proprietorship in an organization. It qualifies you to be part of a company's income and resources.

Simply put, stocks are one way to build wealth, raise money for funding products, growth, and other initiatives.

Immediately after, the end of the industrial age- where money was primarily made by the aristocratic capitalists who owned all the big businesses; which were generally in charge of providing jobs to the population, was met with the beginning of the information age. The professionals had made a resemblance of the kind of paper assets which were exclusively meant for the bourgeois, available to all, who had put away enough cash to turn into a capital in the form of portfolios. Thus, the information age saw the birth of a new class. The class of investors who, by accessing information about various industries, were able to buy into a new income stream.

Purchasing stock gives an investor a share in the industry that they have bought into, even though it does not guarantee returns.

This is the reason for the statement that investment is risky. Before any standard investment, even in modern times, a potential stock investor is aware of the risk that they're taking on. Even though the industry which they are buying into would do what they can within legal limits, to convince them of the prospect of profit with them.

This convincing, of the financially literate, is done by means of presenting cash balance sheets and periodical fiscal performances. Speculations are then made by the potential stock investor, according to the information they've received from the available material.

A different type of stock is known as favored stock. This kind of stock grants profit sharing on the buyer without granting them democratic rights, useful for decision-making in the internal affairs of the industry into which they've bought.

Previously, investors usually get a paper stock testament - called a security – which confirmed the quantity of offers claimed in each stock purchase. Today, share proprietorship is typically recorded electronically, and the offers are held in the road name by your financier firm.

Another fact is putting away, which involves setting aside cash to contribute. This means building up an enhanced portfolio. Portfolios should be balanced intermittently depending on life changes, yet the attention ought to stay on the long haul. Proper investment is done with the end in mind, and this means regular checks and updates, which some industries aid by sending out periodicals to their shareholders to keep them abreast of developments relevant to their involvement in stock.

Before you take that first step

"The secret to investing is to figure out the value of something – and then pay a lot less."

Joel Greenblatt

It is essential to ace the nuts and bolts before you proceed to purchase your first stock. However, this may not make you an extraordinary financial specialist overnight but having the understanding of the rudiments of stock investment will grant you the ability to figure out how to put resources into stocks with certainty.

•   Take inventory of your present financial situation

Likewise, before you settle on any contributing choice, plunk down and investigate your whole financial road map - mainly if you've never made a monetary arrangement.

A brief historical background to investing

After the cold war, there arose a need to protect would-be investors from hanging themselves at the stock market square. This could occur when individuals are allowed to take on investment options with capital requirement levels that may not be sustainable by their current financial situations. The Securities Exchange Commission, which had been set in 1934, then set a cap on investment limits for individuals and couples.

In the bestselling guidebook for investment- Rich Dad's Guide to Investing, which is an installment in his Rich Dad series. Robert Kiyosaki discusses how he struggled through the phase of coming to understand why his childhood friend would refuse to let him in on the kinds of investment opportunities he invested in to produce outstanding results.

The regulations of the SEC thus brought to light what he identified in his book series as the different classes of investors. These classes are stated below:

The Accredited investor- Who invests mainly because they meet the cashflow/capital requirement to purchase big-time stock investment options.

The Sophisticated investor- Who invests using their notable knowledge of how the markets worked. This Enabled them to form smart opinions about where the markets would go, given various situations.

The Inside investor- Who creates business enterprises that offer stock options to the market, thus automatically qualifying them to be both accredited investors and big business owners with corporate governing power.

The Ultimate investor- These are those who become selling shareholders.

Additionally, the initial step to fruitful stock contribution is making sense of your objectives and hazard resistance. This is either all alone or with the assistance of a money related proficient. There is no assurance that you'll bring in cash from your ventures. However, when you get the realities about sparing and contributing and finish a savvy plan, you ought to have the option to increase monetary security throughout the years and appreciate the advantages of dealing with your cash.

Setting good objectives would include taking into thought on what type of profits you intend to make, and then learning enough about investment trends in the market. This will enable you to determine the right investment options that will help you go from where you are in your finances to where you have decided to be. This is why investment options are also sometimes referred to as investment vehicles; they help you to move from where you are to where you want to be.

Take note of these Significant realities

•   Before you make sense of your system, take a few notes about your money related circumstance and objectives.

•   Value putting expects financial specialists to stay in it as long as possible and to apply exertion and research to their stock determination.

•   Investors who follow development systems should be careful of official groups and news about the economy.

•   Momentum financial specialists purchase stocks encountering an upturn may decide to short-sell those protections.

•   Dollar-cost averaging is the act of making normal interests in the market after some time.

Conventional approach to investing in stock?

The best thing about stock trading or investment methodologies is that they're adaptable. On the off chance that you pick one, and it sometimes falls short for your hazard resistance or calendar, you can make changes. However, be admonished: doing so can be costly. Each purchase conveys a charge. All the more critically, selling resources can make an acknowledged capital increase. These increases are assessable and, in this manner, costly.

Before you start to look into your venture procedure, it's imperative to assemble some essential data about your monetary circumstance. Ask yourself these fundamental inquiries:

•   What is your current money related situation?

•   What is your average cost for basic items, including month to month costs and obligations?

- How much would you be able to stand to contribute—both at first and on an on-going premise?

Even though you don't need to be bothered with a ton of cash to begin, you should avoid the impulse of getting started based on the off chance that you cannot stand to do much in the market, thereby settling for only the small scale investment options. In the event that you have a lot of obligations or different commitments, consider the effect that investing will have on your circumstance before you begin setting cash aside. This will help you to set perspective and to determine worthwhile objectives in your investment plan.

Next, set out your objectives. Everybody has various requirements, so figure out what you are. Is it proper to say that you are aiming to put something aside for retirement? Is it right to say that you are hoping to make large buys like a home or vehicle later on? On the other hand, would you say you're putting something aside for your kids' instruction? This will help you narrow down a methodology as having a goal for your investment intentions is crucial to deciding the

investment options that you will take, not to mention, that will suit your cause.

Check out what your hazard resilience is. This is typically controlled by a few key variables, including your age, salary, and to what extent you have until you resign. The more youthful you are, the more hazard you can take on. More risk implies more significant yields, while lower chance methods increases won't be acknowledged as fast. Be that as it may, remember, high-chance speculations likewise mean there's a more prominent potential for misfortunes also.

Several tales of woe in investing have occurred because investors got greedy or became emotional in their pursuit, and this led them to pursue hot tips with astronomical promises of yields in investment opportunities, which required them to invest hazardous amounts of capital. The hazard in investing is hardly ever the amount to be invested, but the financial situation of the investor who is getting involved in the investment option.

Warren Buffet, an American business magnate and Philanthropist who happened to be one of the greatest investors alive today, said that he regularly goes into investment floors, not to see who won, but to take note of those who lost money. He wanted to know what they did wrong. So, that he could be better informed on how not to tow the lines that they did, it is true that in investing, you only need to be right once.

However, there can be dire consequences following losses that prove too great, depending on the financial situation of the investor.

Finally, it is a great idea to become familiar with the nuts and bolts, which is the language and operations of investing. This is the beginning of what it means to be financially literate. It is a smart thought to have an essential comprehension of what you're getting into, so you're not contributing aimlessly. Pose inquiries. Also, read on to find out about a portion of the key systems out there.

CHAPTER TWO

THE SECRET SAUCE TO INVESTMENTS

"Games are won by players who focus on the playing field- not by those whose eyes are glued to the scoreboard."

Warren Buffet

Do you know that everyone invests? How you may ask me? Investments is not only tied to money, but also to time, effort, health, job, business and career. While these forms of investing are aimed at one goal, most of them have a link that is directed to the future.

From an investment analyst on Wall Street to every stay-at-home- mom, we are investing. When you spend time to obtain a degree from college so that you stand a chance to get employed in the future, you're investing in your career. Taking out time to attend conferences and business summits that will boost your career, is investing in your business. As you take time to engage in healthy exercises every morning or evening regularly, you're investing in your health. When you take out time with your family to see the beauty of nature in a tourist field, you're investing in your family.

Several people reap the richest rewards from their investments after retirement. Since investing in these kinds, investments have great returns in the future- how much more making a commitment to invest with your finances.

Here in this chapter, we'll be looking at what investment is and some key terms about investment. Truthfully, the sooner you start to plan, the better off you'll be in the future.

What is investment?

An investment is an asset procured with the objective of creating pay or appreciation. In a monetary sense, an investment is the acquisition of merchandise that are not expended today but are utilized later on to make riches. In fund, speculation is a money related resource bought with the possibility that the advantage will give pay later on at a more significant expense for a benefit.

A stock or a bond is an investment. Individuals are presently urged to make interests in their vehicles and even their level of screen televisions. These things may bode well; however, they should be carefully, ventured into.

For instance, your investment for today (time, cash, exertion, and so on) whereby you expect a more remarkable result later on, which includes what was initially placed in.

Also, investing involves putting cash to work to begin or extend a venture or to buy an advantage or premium. Thereafter, those assets are then set to work, with the objective of generating cash flow, and other incentives after some time. The expression "venture" can allude to any instrument utilized for creating future pay. In the money related sense, this incorporates the acquisition of securities, stocks, or land property among a few others. Moreover, a developed structure or other office used to create products can be viewed as speculation. The creation of merchandise required to deliver different products may likewise be considered as a contributing factor.

Making a move with expectations of raising future income can likewise be viewed as speculation. For instance, when you decide to seek extra training, the objective is regularly to build information and improve abilities with expectations of creating more salary. Since contributing is arranged toward future development or salary.

There's a chance related to interest in the situation that it doesn't work out or misses the mark.

For example, putting resources into an organization that winds up failing or an undertaking that comes up short. This is the thing that isolates contributing from sparing - setting aside is gathering cash for some time later that isn't in danger, while the venture is giving cash something to do for future addition and involves some hazard.

Venture and Monetary Development

Financial development can be supported using sound ventures at the business level. At the point when an organization builds or gains another bit of creating hardware so as to raise the yield of merchandise inside the office, the expanded creation can cause the country's total national output (Gross domestic product) to rise. This permits the economy to develop through expanded creation dependent on the past gear venture.

Also, building and running a successful business venture does have its string of benefits for would-be investors. Investing as a business venture comes with tax advantages because the assets purchases would be done in the name of an entity that is already responsible for contributing to the GDP of the state in which the business is located. Profits that are made as an individual, which include ordinary earned income, i.e., salaries, sole proprietorship earnings, etc., are highly susceptible to heavy taxation.

There is also the advantage, as mentioned in the previous chapter, of qualifying automatically as an accredited investor. Once your business goes public and begins to offer stocks to the market, thus providing an opportunity for others to create wealth using your venture as an investment vehicle. The economic system is designed to reward investors whose path to creating wealth allows for others to tag along.

Of course, the expertise and experience that would come to play to create and maintain a thriving business would also be of great use in determining what investment options would be safe for you to invest your cash. The statement, "It takes one know one," is highly relevant in the world of investment.

The IS-LM model, which means "speculation reserve funds" (IS) and "liquidity inclination cash supply" (LM), is a Keynesian macroeconomic model that shows how increments in a venture at a national level mean increases in monetary interest and the other way around.

Why do you need to invest?

Investing permits you to place your cash in channels that can possibly gain solid paces of return. Investing is the art of multiplying your money by putting it aside your businesses and ventures that you do not need to know much about.

Except for the fact that you have the prospect of realizing profit, adjudged by looking at their financial statements, so that you can make money even while you sleep.

When you invest, you have ensured that the people behind the venture are aware of what they are doing. You only determine how likely the venture is to make a profit, where the type of profit that you're likely to realize from the venture would fit into your financial plan, and then watch the numbers roll in.

On the probability that you don't invest, you are passing up chances to expand your money-related worth. Evidently, you can lose your cash in speculations, yet on the off chance that you invest astutely, the possibility to pick up cash is higher than if you never invest. Investing ought to be seen as the best way to save money.

Motivations to enable you to put away your cash Develop your cash

Putting away your cash for investment will permit you to develop it. Most venture vehicles, for example, stocks, endorsements of the store, or securities, offer profits for your cash over the long haul. This arrival permits your cash to construct, making riches after some time.

Since cash stacked away in the banks is continuously being threatened by inflation and devaluation, it just makes more financial sense to ensure that your money is bound upwards in the value curve. For instance, heirs who have inherited only cash from their benefactors cannot be compared to those who have been left with portfolios of stocks and estate.

The difference is that assets tend to rise in value while whole cash is perishable, even before spending begins. It would take this type of reasoning and understanding to comprehend why a known punishment for rich kids who don't behave is to have them expunged from the family estate while they are paid off by a one-time lump sum.

Put something aside for retirement

Conduct a little experiment in your home. Wake up one morning and strap or tie a heavy household object to your body and proceed to do the things that you do in your everyday life. Brush your teeth, take a bath, make breakfast, etc., Notice the increased difficulty that you experience in getting your routine done. This has become the reality of folks who do not understand that they simply would have all the energy of their youth to continue to earn a wage with it.

At around the middle of the 20th century, the promise of job security and retirement benefits just don't exist as they once did. This means that companies no longer have the responsibility of catering for their employees when some of them are due for retirement. It's up to you to prepare for your own retirement and have the lifestyle that you want to have in your advanced years.

As you work and continue to make ordinary earned income in the form of salaries and wages, you ought to set aside some finances for retirement. Put your future reserve funds into an arrangement of investments.

For example, stocks, securities, shared assets, land, organizations, or valuable metals. At that point, at retirement age, you can live off assets earned from these investments.

In the light of your resistance of hazard, you might need to consider playing it less safe at a more youthful age with your investments. More serious hazard expands your odds of winning more prominent riches. Getting progressively moderate with your ventures as you become more established can be insightful, particularly as you're close to retirement age.

Gain better yields

To develop your cash, you have to place it in a position where it can acquire a high pace of return. The higher the pace of return, the more cash you'll acquire. Investment vehicles will, in general, offer the chance to gain higher paces of return than investment accounts. In this manner, if you need the opportunity to win a better yield on your cash, you should investigate putting away your cash.

Nonetheless, it pays to create an investment plan and to stick with it. You do not want to concede hyper-costly losses pursuing astronomical yields prompted from a hot tip, or from chasing the new miracle on 31st street, or for fear of being late to the party, investing in a volatile new option and then having your cash crash as the bubble bursts.

President of the United States and Real Estate mogul, Donald Trump, in his book called "The Art of the Deal," recounts an instance during which he received a call from an acquaintance of his. His acquaintance asked that he should invest 50 million dollars in an exclusive new investment opportunity, which would quadruple his investment in a mega yield. After some speculation and thought, he

turned down the offer, and soon after, news came that the real estate opportunity had gone bust, taking with it all the money that was invested by those who bought into it. He said this to mean; sometimes, the best investments are the ones that you do not make.

Arrive at money related objectives

Investing can assist you to achieve enormous money related objectives. In the event that your cash is acquiring a higher pace of return than an investment account, you will gain more cash both over the long haul and inside a quicker period. This arrival on your speculations can be utilized toward major money related objectives, for example, purchasing a home, purchasing a vehicle, going into business, or setting up your kids for school.

A major difference between how the rich buy their personal property and afford running costs and how others do it is that the rich do not like to spend directly on them, even though they have the raw cash to afford it.

For example, if your objective is to buy a new home, set up an investment portfolio towards that end, and begin filling it up with investment vehicles.

These investments can generate enough profit to buy your new home so that you do not need to take a financial setback in order to fulfill your objective. A great advantage of doing things this way is that you would never have to worry about how much anything costs anymore. For you, it would only be a question of what investment vehicles you should be getting your hands on in order to generate the kind of profit required to make the purchase.

Expand on pre-charge dollars

Some investment vehicles permit you to invest your pre-charge dollars. This alternative allows you to set aside more cash for

investment on credit, than if you just went ahead to invest your post- charge dollars.

Leveraging is a big-time advantage to maximize in the world of investment. Taking leverage will allow you, within the reasonable risk that can be allotted to your current financial standing, to accelerate your profit scale. In other words, an investment option that could have taken you a quarter of a year to successfully execute could be fast-tracked and done within a month or less, depending on the unique vehicle, and the amount of leverage that you draw out.

Meet all requirements for boss coordinating projects

A few bosses offer to coordinate the cash you put resources into your 401(k) A company-sponsored retirement account plan up to an exact sum. Obviously, the main way you can qualify and procure these coordinating assets is in the event that you're effectively putting resources into your plan. In this manner, numerous individuals put resources into their 401(k)s to pick up the coordinating manager reserves.

Begin and extend a business

Investing is an important piece of business creation and extension. Various financial specialists like to assist business visionaries and add to the creation of new openings and new items. They appreciate the way towards making and setting up a new organization and building them into fruitful elements that can equip them with profit for their speculation.

A major function of an entrepreneur is raising the capital to execute ideas. Venture capitalists and professional investors have the job of investing money into viable business ideas and existing ventures which have already proven their worth and are in need of funds for expansion. This is why it is possible for you to turn your money over to such professionals who will seek out worthwhile ventures to put your money in for you. This is a good choice for investors who do not have the financial literacy skills required for entering the capital

market on their own and have not yet determined to acquire the skills.

Types of investment

As you have now learned, there are different investment vehicles for fulfilling different investment objectives. The subject of "investment" scares many individuals because it can seem a tad overwhelming, learning to invest, and learning to do it safely. There is a great deal of choices, and it tends to be difficult to make sense of which speculations are directly for your portfolio. The following will walk you through 5 of the most well-known kinds of investment, as well as help you clarify why you might need to consider remembering them for your portfolio.

Stocks

Stocks might be the most notable and straightforward kind of venture. At the point when you purchase stock, you're purchasing a proprietorship share in a traded on an open market organization. A significant number of the greatest organizations in the nation — think General Engines, Apple, and Facebook —

are traded on an open market, which means you can purchase stock in them.

At the point when you purchase a stock, you're trusting that the cost will go up so you would be able to sell it for a benefit. The hazard, obviously, is that the cost of the stock could go down, in which case you'd lose cash. Agents offer stocks to speculators. You can either decide on an online business firm or work up close and personal with a representative.

Bonds

At the point when you purchase a security, you're basically loaning cash to a substance. By and large, this is a business or an administration element. Organizations issue corporate securities, while nearby governments issue metropolitan securities. The U.S. Treasury issues treasury bonds.

After the security develops — that is, you've held it for a foreordained measure of time — you procure back the key you spent on the security, in addition to a decided place of intrigue.

The pace of return for bonds is commonly a lot lower than it is for stocks. However, bonds additionally will, in general, be a lower chance. There is some hazard required, obviously. The organization you purchase a bond from could crease, or the administration could default. Treasury bonds, particularly, be that as it may, are viewed as extremely sheltered speculation.

Common Assets

A common Asset is a pool of numerous financial specialists' cash that is put extensively in various organizations. Shared assets can be effectively overseen or inactively oversaw.

An effectively overseen support has a reserve chief who picks organizations and different instruments in which to put financial specialists' cash. Asset supervisors attempt to beat the market by picking speculations that will increment in esteem. A latently overseen support tracks a significant securities exchange list like the Dow Jones Mechanical Normal or the S&P 500. Some common assets put uniquely in stocks, others just in bonds, and some in a blend of the two.

Shared finances convey a large number of indistinguishable dangers from stocks and bonds, contingent upon what they put resources into. The hazard is less, however, in light of the fact that the speculations are naturally enhanced.

Exchange-Traded Fund (ETF)

Exchange-Traded Fund (ETF) is like common assets, which are an assortment of speculations that track a market record. In contrast to shared assets, which are bought through a store organization, ETFs are purchased and sold on the securities exchanges. Their cost vacillates all through the exchanging day, while common supports' worth is just the net estimation of your ventures.

ETFs are frequently prescribed to new financial specialists since they're more differentiated than singular stocks. You can additionally limit hazards by picking an ETF that tracks a wide record.

Declarations of Store

A declaration of the store (Album) is extremely okay speculation. You give a bank a specific measure of cash for a foreordained measure of time. At the point when that timespan is exhausted, you recover your head, in addition to a foreordained measure of intrigue. The more drawn out the advance time frame, the higher your loan fee.

There are no significant dangers to Discs. They are FDIC (Federal Deposit Insurance Cooperation)-guaranteed up to $250,000, which would cover your cash regardless of whether your bank fails in its obligation. All things considered, you need to make sure you won't need the cash during the term of the Compact disc, as there are significant punishments for early withdrawal.

CHAPTER THREE

OPTION TRADING - A KEY TO SUCCESS

"Risk comes from not knowing what you are doing."

Warren Buffet

Just like you have a choice when offered various options, you can either go for some items while you leave the rest, in the same way, you can deal with trading an option or otherwise. Odds are you might want to inquire about each teeny-weeny bit of variety placed before you, but you still have to choose. Even without all relevant information about the item, you have to pick your options, eventually. Most of the time, when you are aware of the potential of your choice of an item over another – probably it'll better serve a bogging purpose – you are limiting chances of making risky choices.

This chapter provides information on what options trading entails. You'll get to know the kinds of options available and how they can open you up to success in the market.

What is an Option?

An option is an agreement that gives the purchaser right, yet not the commitment, to purchase (on account of a call) or sell (on account of a put) the basic resource at an agreed-upon price and date.

Options exchanging may appear to be overwhelming from the outset, yet it is a straightforward venture on the off chance that you know a couple of key focuses. Financial specialist portfolios generally get built with a few resource classes. These might be stocks, securities, ETFs, and even shared assets. Options are another benefit class, and when utilized effectively, they offer numerous favorable circumstances that exchanging stocks and ETFs alone do not.

Fundamentally, trading in options will allow you to grow your funds by putting to work any technical know-how that you have of the financial markets. These skills will help you largely to predict the rise and falls, known as bullish and bearish movements in the curve.

The terms "bullish" and "bearish" are terms used to refer to the current trend of the market, whether prices are rising or falling, hence, whether it is advisable to buy or to sell. The bullish movement means that the price of an option is rising because investors are buying more and more of it. It is derived from the upward movement of the bull's horns when goring, hence it is used to refer to a raise. The bearish movement is derived from the downward swipe of a bear's arms when it claws at something, and so, it is used to refer to a fall in the price of an option because traders are buying less and less of it.

There are some irregularities, however, in options trading, such as inside trading. This is when a big-time member of a company that is currently offering an investment option goes ahead to purchase those options, with a look to outplay the very investors who are, in essence, lending their money to the company by means of public buy-in.

Such an irregularity could be tempting to insiders because the game of options trading is one of insight. The ones who know more about the market, and as such, are able to foretell its movements beyond mere open speculation, usually outclass those who enter the market with nothing but cash and hope to make huge returns. It is the acquisition of this skill set, as well as the language of the trade that has made the investment vehicle of options trading appear rather daunting to beginners.

However, there are several means by which to quickly equip oneself, with the requisite skillset and knowledge base, to begin trading options. In fact, modern option brokers will typically allow beginners to practice using dummy accounts which contain what could be referred to as hypothetical money so that they can test their newly acquired skills and have a feel of the reins of the market, just before they then proceed to use their actual funds in the live options trading market.

Merging your funds to a host or professional account so that your funds are automatically traded for you by a professional is also an option. Usually, such a professional that you select will be entitled to an agreed percentage of your profits when you make a killing in the market, just like turning your money over to a professional investor when investing in other investment vehicles such as bonds, ETF's, etc.

A Fundamental Difference

In the world of investing, there exists a slight yet crucial difference in how you can choose to function in the market. You can decide to largely be a fundamental investor, using what is known as fundamental analysis to probe investment options, or a technical investor, who will use technical readings and an acquired ability to understand them, to predict market movements in order to make a profit.

A fundamental investor possesses the financial literacy to adjudge an investment option or opportunity by paying attention to such elements as the balance sheets of businesses that are being considered for investment, operational styles and practices and the nuts and bolts of running a successful business venture. To the fundamental investor, the internal performance of the business will determine whether or not their investment offering is good enough or not.

Option trading deals mainly with technical analysis, that is, the technical investor. In order for you to be a technical investor, you need to learn and understand how trends and external behaviors, in terms of market readings, typically affect stock performance (sp) so that you can tell whether prices will rise or fall. Hence, you can know whether you should buy or sell.

A technical investor has the financial literacy skills to pay attention to elements including current foreign and international policy, international relations, political climate, current consumer behavior, security in the location of the business rendering the stock option, etc.

Key Takeaways

Here are a few caveats to take notice about option trading.

People use alternatives for money, to estimate, and to support chance.

Options are known as subordinates since they get their incentive from a hidden resource.

An investment opportunity contract commonly speaks to 100 portions of the underlying stock; however, choices might be composed of any kind of fundamental resource from securities to monetary standards to wares.

The rights of option: buyers have rights, sellers have obligations.

The privileges of option: purchasers have rights, choice dealers have commitments.

Types of Option

There are just two kinds of options—calls and puts. Call and put alternatives are an immediate type of speculation and ought to be viewed in that capacity. You can accomplish all that you need on a venture premise with options, similarly as you would with any stock, security, or common reserve. That reality is critical to recall.

Each position is fabricated utilizing alternatives made out of all calls, all puts, or a blend of the two. One thing that shrewd alternative brokers know is that you can sell choices as effectively as you get them. That will be one of the primary topics of this book as you will before long observe that a larger part of my exchanges involves the selling of alternatives.

Try not to worry on the off chance that you've heard that selling alternatives is hazardous. The way that I do it has restricted hazards. One of the extraordinary viewpoints about the monetary markets is that you can sell something first that you don't possess yet. Rather than the standard thing "purchase low, sell high," we can invert it and "sell high, purchase low." Right now, the deal exchange comes first.

How Call and Put Choices Work

Alternatives are another type of speculation that can be purchased and sold simply like a stock, a bond, or an item. They are alluded to as "subsidiary" speculations because a choice's worth is gotten from different sources, which we will discuss later on in the book. On the off chance that you've perused a portion of the standard writing that is distributed about choices, you will see the models given from the purchaser's perspective available. I need to tell you that I'm going to instruct you to exchange from the short side (selling) just as the long side (purchasing) of a choice contract. Why constrain yourself to one procedure?

Calls

A call option gives the holder a right to buy a stock. When you place an order to buy stock in a trading session, it is known as a call. This, however, in today's option trading practice, can be done digitally, that is, without an actual phone call. Buying an option is known as going long on it.

Puts

A put option gives the holder the right to sell a stock. Think of a call option as a down-payment for a future purpose. When you sell an option, you are said to have gone short on it.

How Accomplish Option Works

A purchaser of a call alternative has the desire that the hidden security is going to climb. Stating "hidden security," I'm alluding to the stock or product where you are exchanging choices on.

A call purchaser has the option to control a bullish directional situation of long 100 portions of stock (in the instance of investment opportunities) for a predetermined timeframe (until choice lapse day) at a specific strike value level (the cost at which you will purchase the stock). The purchaser pays an expense to the option vendor for this right, which is known as the "premium."

On account of item choices, the call purchaser has the privilege to control one long fates contract for a predefined timeframe at a specific strike value level. The purchaser has no commitment to practice the alternative agreement and transform it into a bullish situation in the basic security on the off chance that it isn't gainful to do as such.

CHAPTER FOUR

HOW TO TRADE WITH THE TREND

Have you been wondering what is the best time to sell or buy options? What time particularly guarantees maximum outcome when you invest in an option? Although trends do not last in the long run, it is impossible to deny the profits available to traders if effectively used while in vogue. Trading options with the trend is of massive advantage to the market.

In this chapter, I present how you can trade with the trend, buy and sell options, purchase calls, and puts. You'll understand how to send put options and make profit irrespective of the market, and how to put your knowledge into practice.

Buying Options Versus Selling Options

From dynamic hypotheses to hazard, the executives and merchants exploit the fascinating adaptability of alternatives on a normal premise. Be that as it may, rather than traditional fates items, exchanging alternatives requires more skill. We should look at the mechanics of purchasing and selling alternatives contracts.

Purchasing Calls and Puts

Regardless of what item you're exchanging, purchasing and selling are ordinarily the two fundamental activities. In many markets, when a purchase request is executed, another long position is opened. For a sell, either a current long is short, or another short position is made at a showcase. These activities are a basic piece of the fates, money, and value exchanges.

By correlation with progressively customary protections, the use of alternatives is extraordinary. While the facts confirm that purchasing and selling alternatives contracts are key components of dynamic exchanging, each might be cultivated from multiple points of view utilizing calls and puts. Here is a speedy breakdown of each:

Calls: The purchaser of a call choice has the privilege to buy the agreement's basic resources at a predefined cost (for example, strike cost) at the very latest an approaching date in time.

Puts: The purchaser of a put alternative has the option to sell the agreement's basic resources at a particular cost at the very latest an expected date in time.

At a point when you purchase a call or put alternative, the premium is the cost paid for the chance to execute the agreement as indicated by its details. The premium is the risk accepted by the dealer: If an advantageous move-in cost esteems an agreement to be "in cash," a monetary benefit might be made sure about simply after the premium is surpassed.

Call Options: Buying Versus Selling

Previously, we have seen that a call option, alluded to as a "call," is a type of subordinate contract that gives the consider option purchaser the right. Yet not the commitment, to purchase a stock or other money-related instrument at a particular cost – the strike cost of the alternative – inside a predetermined time allotment.

The vender of the alternative is committed to offering security to the purchaser if the last choose to practice their choice to make a buy. The purchaser of the option can practice the alternative whenever preceding a predetermined termination date.

The termination date might be three months, a half year, or even one year later on. The merchant gets the price tag for the choice, which depends on how close the alternative strike value is to the cost of the hidden security at the time the choice is bought, and to what extent a timeframe stays till the option's termination date.

As it were, the cost of the alternative depends on how likely, or improbable; it is that the option purchaser will get an opportunity to gainfully practice the option preceding lapse. Generally, choices are sold in loads of 100 offers.

The purchaser of a call alternative looks to make a benefit if and when the cost of the fundamental resource increments to a cost higher than the choice strike cost. Then again, the dealer of the call option expects that the cost of the benefit will decrease, or if nothing else, never ascend as high as the choice strike/practice cost before it lapses. Thereby, the cash got for selling the choice will be an unadulterated benefit.

In the event that the cost of the fundamental security doesn't increment past the strike value before termination, at that point, it won't be gainful for the option purchaser to practice the alternative, and the choice will lapse useless, "out of the cash."

The purchaser will endure a misfortune equivalent to the cost paid for the call option. Then again, if the cost of the basic security

transcends the option strike value, the purchaser can productively practice the option.

Put Options: Buying Versus Selling

Selling put options gives market players the option to gain bullish exposure, and this might be due to the security in question, at some time in the future, at a price beneath the current market price, as an added benefit.

When you buy a put option, you have the right to sell a security at a predetermined price. However, when you sell a put option, you have an obligation to buy the security at a predetermined price to the option buyer.

How to Sell Put Options and Make Profit

As an option trader, you should sell puts only if you are comfortable with owning the underlying security at the predetermined price. This is because when you sell, you are assuming an obligation to buy   if the counterparty chooses to sell.

In addition, it would only make sense to enter trades at a time when there is an attractive price to be paid for the stock. This is the most crucial thing to consider when selling puts under any market conditions. There are other benefits of selling puts, and they can be exploited once this important pricing rule is satisfied. The ability to generate portfolio income is paramount because, in the event that the initial capital expires without being put to use by the counterparty, the seller retains the initial capital. Besides, there is also the benefit of selling puts the occasion to own the basic security at a price below the present market price. This means a cost-effective way to enter the market with the put option that you sell.

The Practice of Put Selling

Let us examine an example from Investopedia, a leading digital source of financial education, of prudent put selling. Shares offered by Company 1 are currently attracting investors with higher profitability prospects due to its new line of stock. Let's say the stock is currently selling at $270, and the ratio of price-to- earnings currently sits under 20, which is a reasonable valuation when you consider this company's rapid growth. If you are optimistic about their prospects, you may go bullish and buy 100 shares for

$27,000, including payable fees and commissions. As an alternative, one could choose to sell a put option in January for $250, expiring two years from now at just $30.

What this means is that the stock option's expiry will be the 3rd Friday of January, two years from now, and has an exercised price of $250.

By choosing to sell this option, you agree to make a purchase of about 100 shares of Company 1 for $250 no later than January, two years from now. Clearly, since shares offered by Company 1 are currently trading for $270, the put buyer is not going to ask you to make a purchase of the shares for $250. This means that you will collect the premium while you wait.

However, if the stock drops to $250 in January, two years from now, you will be vital to buy the 100 shares at that price, but you will keep the premium of $30 per share so that your net cost will be $220 per share. If, on the other hand, the price of the shares does not fall to

$250, the option will expire worthlessly, and you will keep the entire

$3,000 premium.

In summary, as an alternative to buying 100 shares for $27,000, you may choose to sell the put and reduce your safety net cost to $220 per share. In the event that the stock option expires valueless, you will reserve the right to keep the $30 initial capital paid on each share, thus representing a 12 percent profit, when you bought at

$250.

With this, you can now see why it is a smart choice to sell puts on securities you want to own. If Company 1 declines, you will be required to part with a sum of up to $25,000 to buy the shares at $250 (since you kept $3,000 premium, your net cost will be $22,000). You should also bear it in mind your broker may force you to sell other holdings to purchase this position if you do not have sufficient cash available in your account to execute the purchase with.

The process of deciding what would be the best time to sell a put is one that requires quite a lot of patience, coupled with an understanding of the long-term risks and rewards that are inherent in the transaction of either option. Therefore, it is a great idea to learn how to wait and watch while carefully deciding what would be the intelligent thing to do while giving attention to the current state of the market that you are trading in stock.

The decision to sell put options can be a smart means of generating some additional income in your portfolio. While also gaining good exposure to securities that you would like to own but on which you also want to limit your initial capital investment spending.

Conclusively, investing is mostly a matter of priority. There can be as many investment plans as there are investors. This variance is desires and objectives, either as a family or as an individual, will be responsible for guiding your mind as an investor in deciding that ride to take, in terms of selecting the right investment vehicle. Your investment plan and choices do not need to be more complicated than they need to be, depending on where you are now and where you want to be in your financial journey.

CHAPTER FIVE

SELLING OPTIONS FOR MONTHLY INCOME

"The intelligent investor is a realist who sells to optimists and buys from pessimists."

-      **Benjamin Graham**

A short-put option (sometimes called a naked option) occurs when an option buyer buys an option (shares or currencies) when the price is lower than its current market price and waits till there is a decrease in the price. Buying a short-put option simply means that the buyer expects that the price of the stock or currency will soon fall or, on the other hand, that the value of the option increases. In essence, the underlying reasoning underlining short-put option trading is that a premium is collected by the writer in expectation of an increase in the price/value of shares optioned.

Meanwhile, a strike price (also called the exercise price) is the price at which an option price is traded.

Let's illustrate short-puts

We shall now proceed with how the short put option strategy works with an example.

Imagine that the current market price of Unilever on the New York Stock Exchange is $100 per share. If it could be reliably predicted that this stock price will increase in the next 30 days, an option buyer can commence a short put option. How?

They will sell at a price (say $5.00) for the next month, making an instant gain of $500 on 100 units of Unilever shares. They will then wait and monitor the market price of the shares until the expiration of the option. If the market price of Unilever shares hovers above the

$100 at the expiration of the option, the total gain of $500 remains with the option buyer fewer commissions.

This summarily closes the option trade. However, a drop in the stock price will mean that the seller can buy back Unilever shares for $100 per share and close the option trade. This will reduce the amount of loss they stand to incur on the option. Failure to buy back options with declining prices early enough will lead to massive loss to the option buyer.

When to use short-puts?

Most often, there are shares that appear over- or underpriced! When you observe such shares for some time, and there exists a high expectation that their prices may increase, that is a good time to short-put. However, in any of these situations, the strike price must have been well established. When a particular share or the stock market is generally experiencing a bullish trend, it is a good time to short-put also.

The process

The beginning of any option trading is to be ready to face risk and uncertainty. This is because prices of shares and currencies are extremely volatile and sometimes produce surprising bubbles. To

start trading options, you need to have a broker with whom you open an online margin account. A margin account is opened to make cash available to buy shares in the event that the price of optioned share falls. Once your margin account is opened, you have to find shares that you reliably expect the price to increase or remain stable within the short time during which the option will expire.

Also, you can spot shares that can be purchased at prices lower than they are currently traded on the Stock Exchange market. You will then have to set a date for the expiration of the proposed option contract. The date is usually between 30 to 90 days. Next is for you to agree on the strike price and then sell the put, after which your account is credited with your earnings on the put. If the shares put on option closes at a price higher than the strike price, you remain the owner of the credit. The reverse will be the case in the event that the option price at expiration falls below the strike price, in which case, the option seller will have to buy back the option.

Short-put strategies

Let us discuss a few short put strategies here:

i.   Long Call: A long call short-put option occurs when an option is bought in the open market with the expectation that the value of the security will increase within the option duration.

ii.   Short Put Ladder: This is when an investor sells "one in-the- money put option," buys "one at-the-money put option" and still buys another "out-of-the-money put option," a strategy that is particularly suitable when there is an expectation that a share's price will "bubble up" within a very short time. An "in-the-money" buy is a situation when the spot rate falls short of the strike price, whereas an "at-the-money" buy arises when the strike price and the spot rate are the same when the option expires. An "out-of- the-money" scenario is when the spot rate is greater than the strike price. The reverse would be the cases if the options were the on-call basis.

iii.   Short Put Butterfly: This involves selling a "one in-the-money put option," buying "two at-the-money put options," and then selling a "one out-of-the-money put option." This strategy is usually employed by risk-averse option traders though the limited risk also means the returns on it will be limited.

Short-put: why go for it

Two main reasons encourage investors to short-put, but all is about returns. First, the option premium is immediate, even before the days start counting. Suffice to say that while waiting for the expiration of the option, the seller can invest the returns from it to generate more income. Second, returns from options are usually significant on a short horizon. Those looking for a quick return on investment usually opt for option trading.

The risks

Generally, option trading is not only speculative but also involves high-risk venturing, notwithstanding that investors do a lot of

technical analysis of stock price behavior before venturing into it. The principle of risk-return trade-off fully applies here. It is needless to say that the volatility and incessant bubbles in stock prices can negatively affect returns and risks associated with security trading.

First, a considerable loss may arise if the price of the security falls sharply due to unforeseen factors, especially in the absence of hedging. In a case of mild or little fall in such price, the writer will still incur some losses by buying the option and re-sell most probably for a loss. Global and national economic downturns, as well as industrial crises, significantly alter share prices of firms.

In conclusion, avoid incurring huge losses, option investors do not only study hard the trend of share prices, but they also hedge against losses.

CHAPTER SIX

RECOGNIZING THE RISKS

"Take risks: if you win, you will be happy; if you lose, you will be wise."

- **Swami Vivekananda**

Life is a risk; living, waking up daily, accepting job offers, quitting relationships can be daunting, and risky, but guess what? You have the ability to take some risk, no matter how high the mountain is, no matter how deep that ocean is, no matter how fiery that fire is. The truth is life is a risk, and making money isn't any easier, is it?

Every one of us wants to make some money, get on the list of one of the richest individuals in our field, and become a force to be reckoned with, and hopefully recognized and mentioned by Forbes one day. None of these dreams, aspirations, and desires will come by without taking a risk, without taking a bold step, even if it means putting all your eggs in one basket. Taking risks is similar to walking through a dark tunnel, with coals of fire on the ground of the tunnel.

Now, imagine that. Would you rather wait behind, and miss a lifetime wealth, and posterity, because you are scared you would burn your feet even before you see the light at the end of the tunnel. Think of this. If you walk through the tunnel, it is your gain, even though you may lose your health for few days, but if you choose to remain at where you are, you will gain nothing more than your perfect health but will lose the opportunity to become a wealthy fellow.

I want you to reminisce carefully on the above analogy; you would most likely not make some impressive paradigm shift in your financial life if you fail to take some risk.

In finance, the risk is defined as the likelihood of occurrence or non- occurrence of return on investment. Risks must be differentiated from uncertainty. While risk can be quantified in probabilistic terms, uncertainty cannot.

For example, the probability that summer will begin earlier than normal cannot be quantified, hence it is uncertain. However, the probability that greater or less than a specified amount given some measurable economic conditions can be ascertained --this is a risk.

In option trading, prospective investors must clearly define the risks attached to the proposed options less they incur huge losses. The whole business of trading in options is denominated by risks. While an option holder risks the possibility of losing all the premium paid, the option writer faces higher risks in the face of highly volatile share prices. Good knowledge of risk components helps the investor to make informed decisions.

Risks involved in Option Trading

"If you don't take risks, you'll never know."

-        Anonymous

For every investment, there is an advantage and disadvantage, and it is necessary that you understand and recognize the risks in option trading. All investments involve one risk or the other. Global events, as well as national and local economic activities, exert great influence on share prices of companies. So, option trading is most times subject to prevailing economic indicators. This is apart from industry and firm-based events that can spur or impair companies' stock prices.

Measuring risks

Measuring risks typically involves applying measures of dispersion from the projection that is, variance. In finance, statistical techniques such as probability, variance, and standard deviations are used to measure investment risks. In most cases, probabilities are attached to the occurrence or otherwise of specified returns. For example, having predicted through technical analysis (such as random walk) that a security price will increase by X in 30 days, a probability of occurrence that ranges from 0 to 1 is attached such that the expected increase does not become probability multiplied by the predicted increase. The expected increase will normally be less than the predicted and hence more reliable.

Types of risk

Broadly, financial experts also distinguish between systematic and unsystematic risks. While the unsystematic risks are those that can be controlled by individual firms, persons and bodies, systematic risks are general or macro in nature and hence cannot be controlled by individual firms or persons. However, further distinctions are necessary for the types of risk that exist

Business and financial risks

Business and financial risks are those related to actual day-to-day operations of a business. These risks are tied to financing, marketing, and human resources activities. Such risks eventually affect share prices since it will affect profitability and dividends.

A good example of business risk is volatility in sales and the possibility of shrinking revenue. Also, a sudden sharp increase in the cost of raw materials, stock-outs, and the problem of illiquidity are risk factors. Financial risk also arises when a company is highly over-levered to the extent that financial obligations are not being met. All these risks affect the value of the firm that is usually expressed as the market price of shares. Business and financial risk can render option trading unprofitable when it causes the share price to fall unexpectedly.

Default risk

Default (or credit risk) refers to the probability that a debtor is unable to repay a debt or its interest. High default risk is a sign of a serious financial problem that can, for example, make borrowers unable to repay bondholders as and when due. Except for gilt-edged securities (government bonds), which are riskless, all other securities, including options, carry with them some elements of default risk. However, the higher the default risk in financial security, the higher the interest payable, but the lesser

investors want to put into it. A bond with a high probability of default is termed a junk bond.

Country and economic risk

The economy of your country has a great effect on how much money you would make from stock trading. Each country and economy have its peculiarities, preferences, and focus; hence financial securities issued in countries differ in characteristics even when they have the same name. Developing and emerging economies, in particular, have higher country risks resulting from legal and institutional structures that may, from time-to-time, exert much influence on share prices. Further, a country that regularly experiences fiscal deficit, high international un-serviced debts will have its securities rated as riskier than others.

Counterparty default risk

Suppose a party to an option arrangement defaults their obligation to the contract due to any reason, does it affect the contract? Yes, it does. All financial securities' arrangements have counterparty risks attached to them. Over-the-counter financial instruments are most susceptible to counterparty risks. There can be several reasons why a party may default in honoring their own part of the contract.

Political risk

Political upheavals, instability and societal disturbances would have a considerable impact on the stock market. A sudden and unexpected change in government, new regulations concerning capital, and money market operations can throw up new risks and uncertainties that will impair stock prices. Essentially, the stock market is very sensitive to information, economic, or political hence, government stance and policies to a great extent dictate share price movement.

Foreign exchange risk

Once you invest in a country other than your own, foreign exchange risk will be tied to such investment. One of the common risks faced by international option writers is foreign exchange risks. The volatile nature of foreign exchange should form the most important decision variable that investors need to consider before venturing into cross-border option trading.

If a Britain decides to write options on a share price of a company listed on the New York Exchange, even if the American firm's share is performing well in the NYSE, there is still a risk inherent in the possibility that the British Pound depreciates in value against the US dollar thereby reducing the returns accruing to the investor.

Liquidity risk

Option trading is premised on principle and assumption that the investor is liquid enough to transact business. Liquidity risk arises when the ability of an investor to have cash to transact business is threatened. To counter this risk, investors will do well by holding other near-money assets to meet cash demand at short notice.

Risk related to interest rate

The interest rate is indirectly related to sharing prices because elementary economic theory posits that when there is a rise in interest rate, demand for shares will fall, and so is the price and vice versa. Interest rate risk arises when there is a sudden unexpected rise in the interest rate that reduces investment in financial securities. Such rise will translate to a fall in demand for shares and hence a fall in share prices. This will have a negative effect on option investors' returns. The best way to invest in securities to counter this risk is to invest when prices and interest rates are low and monitor until prices increase.

Risk of reinvestment

Suppose you re-invest your returns on another highly profitable option now, but there exists no more high yielding opportunity for you to invest when the returns on your former investment accrue. This is a business dilemma called a re-investment risk. The opportunities available may now be yielding far lesser than your initial investment.

Inflation Risk

Inflation affects the value of a country's currency negatively. Inflation risk arises when the worth (value) of return on your investment becomes less due to inflation. The persistent rise in prices erodes the value of the local currency such that a particular amount can no longer buy as much as it would have at the onset of the investment. If your return from an option contract in 90 days' time will be $100. A sudden devaluation of the dollar with the period will make the $100 to have lesser value than it has presently.

Market Risk

Several other factors in the stock market can affect share prices adversely. Market regulations, reforms as well as global political and economic crises can impair share prices and reduce investment value over time.

The risk-return trade-off

The general relationship between risk and expected returns also applies to investment in options. The higher the risk, the higher the expected returns should be. This assertion is correct because the risk is directly proportional to returns since investment with higher risk is expected to generate higher returns.

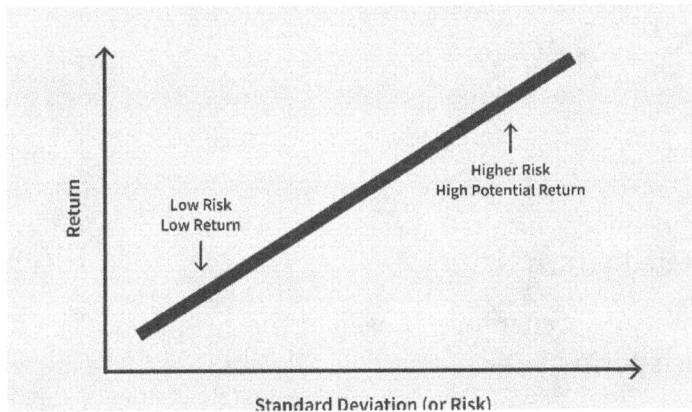

Figure 1: Risk – return trade-off

Figure 1 describes the relationship between risk and returns on investment.

As the risk attached to a particular investment opportunity increases, so does the expected return and vice-versa. The higher you go on the risk/return trade-off curve, the more risk lover you are, and the lower you wish to stay, the more risk-averse you are and the less the expected return.

I need to give a caveat on this assertion! The principle of "the higher the risk, the higher the expected returns" should not be taken as an iconic law as it does not apply in all cases. Take gilt-edged securities (government securities), for example. Such securities are riskless, yet the returns are not only certain, but they are also lucrative even with a zero risk. So, higher risks do not always translate to higher returns on investment.

Expected return

The best way to forecast future events is to attach probabilities to their occurrence. Future returns cannot be predicted with accuracy; hence, in estimating future cash inflows in finance, the probability of such cash flows is used to multiply them. Mathematically, expected return on an investment is the summation of all future cash inflows multiplied by their respective probabilities. Algebraically, we express this relationship as:

$$E(x) = \sum_{i=1}^{n} Pi(Xi)$$

where

E(x) = Expected return

Pi = Probability of occurrence of each of the cash flows Xi = Cash flows for each period

n = period

This means the actual return from an investment at a future date is the summation of all cash inflow accruing on it multiplied by their individual probabilities.

Assignment risk

A seller of an option can be assigned the stock if their option falls within the contract money at the expiration of the option. However, the risk attached to option assignment is that the exact period of assignment is usually beyond the control of the seller, but the closer the option is to its expiration, the higher the risk attached to it.

The assignment of option requires that the buyer exercises the option even though it is not obligatory for them to do so. Let us take an example here: You bought a Coca-Cola 30 days option and today happens to be the expiration day, and the option "is in the money," if it is a naked call, then you have the right buy the shares at the previously agreed strike price. But when it is a naked put, you have the right (but not necessarily the obligation) to sell the shares at a strike price

Selling Puts on high priced stocks

A put share option can get its value from another security, and a call option confers the right to sell at an agreed price (choice exercise price), whereas a put option confers the right to sell the other security at the exercise price on the buyer. Actually, a call option is bullish trading in that the option holder gets more money as the price increases. But a put option is bearish in that the holder only makes more money as the share price goes down.

CHAPTER SEVEN

HOW TO MANAGE AND CONTROL RISKS

"What seems too high and risky to the majority generally goes higher, and what seems low and cheap generally goes lower." – **William O'Neil**

A Right management of your capital and risk exposure is essential in options trading. Managing risk is a part of the market in the stock market. Just like you will buy and sell while you invest, taking a risk should not be a problem. You only have to be on the key as you manage funds effectively. Do not take a risk a risk so big it makes you feel uncomfortable; instead, take a risk you can manage per time. You mustn't expose yourself to unsustainable losses.

Simultaneously, it is advisable to use your investment capital when trading. Do not trade-off with such a capital that you cannot afford to lose. Know the level of risk to which you can expose your fund without having to drown in the flood of loss when it comes sweeping.

Risk is an essential part of the investment. You do not reap where you haven't sown. But by taking drastic steps and careful consideration, you can meaningfully reduce your risk and upsurge your earnings in the market.

Therefore, I'll encourage that you focus on expanding the risk that you may likely face across many sectors. Pick stocks that have factual and accurate forecasts. Take a brief look at the report of your earnings and select those that consistently rise at regular intervals, such as annually and quarterly. Look for low beta stocks (This indicates that the security is less unpredictable than the market) that outperform the market and be cautious of price-to-earnings ratios.

Lastly, add bulk of the value of your stock to your portfolio until you comfortably discern what makes a company proliferate and stand out amongst others in the stock market.

Well, the truth is that investing intelligently isn't that easy. There are some undisputable strategies that we must keep in mind as an

investor when making our investment.

Below are four of the most important strategies that will help to reduce the volatility and risk in your portfolio:

1.   Use of Varied Sectors

Sometimes, you may be remarkably sturdy on the gold sector as you take on precious metal stocks. When gold trades move higher, you'll make incredible gains, but when the prices drop, your whole portfolio will take a massive hit. The challenge about this lies in the lack of differentiated portfolios for various sectors in the industry.

The sectors in Stock market sectors come in different categories; which are: Basic Materials, Technology, Conglomerates, Consumer Goods, Healthcare, Services, and Utilities.

There is nothing wrong with trying to select fascinating stocks. The vital key is to find them in a range of sectors.

For example, gold stocks are found in the basic materials sector, along with silver-based investments, oil, and chemicals. The next step is to Pick the outstanding stocks in this category, ensure that they are few, but do not put everything you have into them.

Instead, reach out to select top-performing stock in consumer goods, just like an up-coming winemaker or manufacturer of a toy. Then carefully scan for a healthcare stock that can successfully treat cancer.

Add up all these, and you'll have a portfolio that has a reduction in downside risk in any sector. Also, you'll find out that your portfolio has less volatility in total since the stocks are not so closely classified within one service or commodity.

In the long run, the best approach to take on is to select enthralling and fascinating stocks across a range of sectors; this will help reduce the possible risk of increasing and dwindling sector momentum. These are taken into consideration because sectors go rise and fall in packs and then drag the whole basket of stocks with them. Therefore, divergence should be used to lessen the whole volatility of your portfolio.

2.   Avoid the Rude shock of Earnings

Does your heart race anytime you hear the report of your earnings that are likely to be announced soon? Do you get tensed up with the fact that you may likely meet or beat the streets?

However, as you desire a positive outcome for your earnings, there are some red flags to watch out for. Many people develop shock when earnings are about to be reported; some others have high blood pressure because of the uncertainty as to whether they will meet or beat the street. Though one may love positive earnings surprises, there is risk associated with such surprises. Such surprises show the inability of the analyst to give the forecast of an accurate record of earning. Besides, surprises are to be anticipated with lower-priced securities, which are intrinsically much riskier.

And so, if your stock earns a large quantity (50 cents to one dollar per share), and analyst forecasts are significantly off the point each quarter, you may also face an increase in risk. This kind of improbability makes it challenging for you to have the confidence to predict how the company will successfully perform in the near future.

Let's take a look at some possible signs that a company may have; this is drawn from the good and bad side.

A limit in Coverage

Not every analyst in a company has the ability to cover the whole stock adequately. This may certainly increase the risk and shocks and surprises in earning.

Inconsistency in Analysis

There is a wide diffusion of analysts' estimates, reflecting the fact that there is a lot of uncertainty about the company's future performance.

New Company

New companies struggle with having a precise estimate for earning records simply because they are new. At this point, surprises are bound to happen, besides there is less or no history to predict future earnings.

Whatever the reason it might be, the risk goes down when there can't be an accurate covering of stock, accurate analysis, and estimate earnings, and few surprises help.

Indispensable Caution with Extremely Low Price/Earning Stocks

It has been verified that some investors usually have the thought that it's an easy task to beat the stock market. Interestingly, I'll advise that you find a stock that trades at an extreme level of a bargain. Therefore, I'll give an illustration of how this can be done.

We will be taking a look at price to earnings ratio (P/E ratio). This simple math is achieved by dividing the price of a share by the amount of earnings per share. If the profit from the earnings of the stock is relatively high compared to its share price, investors that make use of this method usually feel that it's cheap and undervalued. Therefore, new investors may attempt to use this ratio to find out possible hot deals without recognizing they're accidentally increasing their level of risk.

Undeniably, there usually a lure to find out low-priced stocks. Regrettably, in the long run, they are usually anything.

One example is that of Kulicke & Soffa Industries Inc. (NASDAQ: KLIC); who is a lead provider in packaging and involved in packaging electronic assembly solutions.

Recently, in 2010, the stock made $2.00 per share of profit.

However, the share price is only $9.00 which gave a price-earning ratio of 4.7

The average P/E of the industry ratio is 15.3

In the first instance, you might quickly assume that this stock should trade at least three times higher based on this ratio.

However, for several reasons, stocks with unusually low Price/Earnings ratios have been punished by investors. Therefore, from one year to another, earnings could become erratic, or the company may result in a financial relapse with an increase in debt load. Sometimes, it may seem that the stock looks inexpensive based on the Price/Earnings ratio, but as a result of the increase in

the risk of the unknown, investors have taken time to account for this volatility, which is in the form of a lower share price.

Back to the above example

You will find out that KLIC may have a low Price/Earnings ratio, which is based on its volatile earnings, both from the positive and negative angle, over some time. It is probable that in the next quarter, the Price/Earnings ratio may skyrocket for investors if the reports from the company are disappointing.

Therefore, this scenario has made it clear that you'll need to put into consideration other earning ratios instead of focusing on one number or ratio.

For instance, a comparison between the share price of KLIC's and its cash flow per share, and then comparing this to the industry's average, you'll find out that the semiconductor stock is valued fairly. Therefore, the difficulty that analyst faces in assessing future value comes as a result of a wide range of price target that hits from $6 –

$15.

As a result, when a company claims a low P/E ratio, there's often a purpose behind it, which may lead to additional risk in investment.

CHAPTER EIGHT

SELLING PUT OPTIONS

"Never sell yourself short, include your stock."

-   Unknown

Selling put options is known to allow players in the stock market to gain some sort of bullish exposure, with an additional advantage of becoming potential owners of the basic security at a future date at a price that is below the current price in the market.

A basic understanding of what put options entail may be really helpful to you in the quest to understand how selling puts can be of immense benefit to your investment strategy, so we shall examine a typical trading situation as well as possible rewards and risks.

Put Options versus Call Options

Call option, otherwise known as an equity option, is a derivative instrument that gets its value from the fundamental security. Buying an equity option bestows on the holder, the right to own the security at a price that's already predetermined. This price is known as the option exercise price.

On the other hand, a put option bestows on its owner the right to sell the basic security at the option exercise price. Therefore, we can say that when you buy a call option, that is a bullish bet, because the owner makes money if the price of the security goes up while buying a put option is a bearish bet since the owner would make money when the price of the security goes down.

Selling a put or call option can have this directional logic flipped over. More importantly, the holder becomes obligated to the counterparty when selling an option. The reason for this is that it carries a duty to honor the position in case the buyer of such option decides to exercise his or her right to the security outrightly.

Synopsis of buying versus selling options.

When buying a call: Here, you are entitled to buy a security at an already predetermined price.

When selling a call: Here you are obligated to deliver the security at an already predetermined price to the buyer of the option.

When buying a Put: Here, you are entitled to selling a security at a price that is already predetermined.

When Selling a Put: Here, you are obligated to buy the security at an already predetermined price to the buyer of the option.

How to Sell Put Options for Benefit

It is important to note that put options should only be sold if you do not have any issues with owning the underlying security at its predetermined price because you are under an obligation to buy if the counterparty chooses to sell. Also, you should only enter trades that have their underlying security characterized by attractive net prices.

This is just like the most important factor to consider when trying to sell puts profitably in a market environment.

Other benefits of put selling can still be exploited, but that would be after this important pricing condition is met. Your ability to create portfolio income is at the top of this list because the seller would keep the whole premium if the sold put expires without the counterparty exercising his or her right to the security. One other important benefit is that there is an opportunity to own the underlying security at a price that is below the current price in the market.

Practical example of selling Put

Let us examine what it means to actually sell put prudently.

So, let's say we have shares in First Limited Company, and they are great investors, making huge profits from their amazing products. Imagine that their stock is currently trading at say $370 with the price-to-earnings ratio under 20; we can take that to be a reasonable valuation for the fast track the company is taking. So, if you are to be bullish about their prospects, you could buy 100 shares for $37,000, including fees and commissions.

Asides from that, you also have the option of selling a January $350 put option, which is to expire two years from now for just $30. Meaning that the expiration of that option would be the third Friday of January two years from this present time, and it has an exercise price of $350. An option contract covers about 100 shares, so that allows you to collect $3,000 overtime in premium. This excludes commission.

Now, when you sell this option, it simply means you have agreed to buy 100 shares of First Limited Company for $350, and that won't be later than January two years from this present time. So, since the company's shares are currently trading for $370 today, the buyer of the Put won't ask you to buy the shares for $350. So that means you will receive the premium while you are waiting.

If by two years' time (January), the stock has dropped to $350, it means you will have to buy the 100 shares at that price, but you will still keep the premium of $30 per share so that your net cost would become $330 per share. On the other hand, if the shares never fall to $350, the option will expire, and you will have to keep the entire premium of $3,000.

To sum up, another alternative to purchasing 100 shares for $37000, you could also decide to sell the put and have your net cost lowered to $330 per share (or $33000 of the price drops to $350 per share).

So, if the option expires, you would get to retain the $42 per share premium, which is a 12 percent return on a $350 buy price.

Now you can see why it is a wise decision to sell puts on securities you intend owing. If the Company in question declines, it is most likely that you would be required to produce $35,000 to buy the shares at $350.

Don't forget that your broker can force you to sell some of your other holdings in order to take this position if you do not have cash readily available in your account.

So, making a choice of the most appealing time to sell a put requires both patience and a proper understanding of the rewards and risks that take place in the long run.

In conclusion, selling put options can be a very prudent method to create additional portfolio income while you gain exposure to the securities you would like to have under your belt, but still want to control your initial investment.

The concept of Volatility

A statistical measure of the spread of returns for a given market index or security is what is known as volatility. Usually, higher volatility indicates that security is riskier. Volatility is usually measured as the standard error or variance between returns from that same security or market index.

In the markets for securities, volatility is often associated with very notable swings in either direction. For example, when the stock market rises and falls more than one percent over a protracted period of time, that market would be referred to as "volatile." It is important to note that an asset's volatility is a salient factor when pricing options contracts.

To further explain volatility, it often refers to the amount of risk or uncertainty that is related to the size of changes in the value of a security.

Higher volatility simply means that the value of a security can potentially be dispersed over a larger set of values (usually a range). The meaning of this is that the price of the security can change rapidly over a short period of time, and this could happen in either direction. On the other hand, lower volatility means that the value of a security does not fluctuate rapidly or dramatically, and as a result, it tends to be steadier and more stable.

One of the ways to measure the variation of an asset is to quantify its daily returns that are its percentage move on a daily basis.

There is something known as historical volatility. It is a volatility based on historical prices, and it also represents the degree of variableness in an asset's return. Usually, the number is without a unit and is also expressed as a percentage.

So, we can say while the variance is used to capture the spread of returns around the mean of an asset in general, the volatility of that asset is a measure of that variance that is bounded by a specific time period. Therefore, it is possible to report volatility on a daily,

weekly, monthly, quarterly, or annual basis. It is therefore correct to think of volatility as the annualized standard deviation, that is, volatility is equal to the square root of the annualized variance. This is shown as $\sqrt{}$ (variance annualized).

Calculating Volatility

Usually, Volatility is calculated using the variance and standard deviation. The standard deviation is also the square root of the variance.

For example, let's assume we are given monthly stock prices of $1 through $12. With month one as $1, month two as $2, and so on. To calculate the variance, we follow the five steps outlined below

1.   First, we find the average of the data set.

This means we are to add up all the values, and then divide our answer by the number of values. If we add $1, plus $2, plus $3, all the way to up to $12, we will get $78. Then this is divided by 12 since we have 12 numbers in our data set. This provides an average price or means of $6.50

2.   After deriving the mean, we proceed to find the mean deviation. That is the difference between each data value and the mean we derived.

For example, we take $12 - $6.50 = $5.50, then $11 - $6.50 = $4.50. This continues all the way down to our first data value of $1. Note that Negative numbers don't pose any problem. Since we need each value, these calculations can be easily done in a spreadsheet.

3.   Then we square the deviations so that it will eliminate negative values.

4.   Then we add all the squared deviations together. From our example, this equals 92.5.

5.   After adding the squared deviations, we divide the sum of the squared deviations (92.5) by the total number of data values

present, which is 12 in our case.

In this example, the result of our variance is $7.71. Then the square root is taken to get the standard deviation. This would give us

$2.78.

This value of $ 2.78 is a measure of risk and shows how values are dispersed around the average price. It gives the stock traders an idea of how the price may deviate from the mean or average.

Other Measures and Use of Volatility

Another measure of the relative volatility of a particular stock in the market is its beta, denoted by the symbol (β). Usually, a beta (β) approximates the total volatility of the return of security against the returns of a benchmark that the market considers relevant. In most cases, the S&P 500 is used as this benchmark.

One other way to see the volatility of the market is through the Volatility Index, otherwise known as the VIX. The volatility index was crafted by the Chicago Board Options Exchange. Basically, it was a measure to monitor the volatility of the U.S. stock market for an expected period of 30 days against real-time quote prices of the call and put options of the S&P 500.

It is an effective gauge for future investors and traders making investment decisions on the market directions or individual securities. When the reading on the Volatility index is high, it implies that the market is a risky one.

Volatility can also be seen as a variable in the option pricing formulas that shows the extent to which the returns of the basic security will fluctuate between now and the expiration of the option. The volatility is expressed as a percentage coefficient within the formulas for option-pricing, and it arises from trading activities that occur daily. The way volatility is measured will affect the value of the coefficient that is being used.

Finally, Volatility is also useful in pricing options contracts using models like the Binomial tree or the Black Scholes model. The assets that are more volatile would translate to higher options premiums. This is because due to the presence of volatility, there is a great probability that at expiration, the options will end up in-the- money. So, Options traders usually try to predict the future volatility of an asset and so the price of an option in the market somehow reflects its volatility, although in an implied manner.

CHAPTER NINE

ENHANCING A LONG STOCK POSITION

Covered Calls

"More money has been lost trying to anticipate and protect from corrections than actually in them."

-       **Peter Lynch**

Covered calls, also called a "buy-writes" strategy in option trading, occurs when sells options and, at the same time, own the amount of the option instrument. It is a buy-write option strategy when an investor buys the stock when the seller sells the call. The element of "covering" in a covered call is that the shares bought can be delivered to the buyer if and when they exercise. This serves as a sort of protection against risk and volatility. This strategy requires that you own at least 100 units of shares that you are willing to sell (write) in multiples.

Why covered calls?

A distinctive feature of a covered call strategy is the risk reduction element and the limitedness of restrictions on it. This is not to say that covered call is completely risk-free, but that it protects against the unlimited risk of losses if the option is exercised and "in-the-money". Covered calls are particularly suitable for those who want to earn income on the share they own, especially when there are signs that stock price may not rise or that it may even decrease. However, brokers' consent is required before you can employ a covered call strategy for options. Below are two questions that you should ask;

1.   Can I cover call shares I do not own?

Well, yes, but you first need to buy the shares and then re-sell the call.

You must also understand that you may not be able to re-sell the call at the same or higher price you bought it, so there could be a drop in price.

2.   Any inherent risk in covered calls?

The answer here is yes. First, by owning a share means that there exists an original risk in the shares. More than that, you forgo share appreciation by accepting to collect the premium. Even if the share price bubbles positively, you cannot gain more than the agreed strike price because there is a call on the share. This means that holding the share would have been a better option in the case of a sporadic upward swing in its price within the call period. Surprisingly, a fall in the share price also brings some risks for the writer as it could lead to loss beyond what the premium can offset.

My best advice is that you only cover call when sharp bubbles (sporadic swings) are not expected at the price of share within the call period. It is better to be a "bear" in order to trade cover calls

Covered calls tradeoffs

In covered calls trading, two major factors readily pop up for consideration: time and the strike price. Of course, these are the key issues in option trading apart from risk and returns.

- Timing: The farther you are willing to make your covered call, the higher likelihood that you will get a higher premium on the call and vice versa. But the longer the timing, the higher the risk will be attached to the call.
- Strike price: Strike price is a major determinant of a covered call option, and it is also affected by the odds around the success of the call. High-profit odds are associated with "in-the-money" calls while much higher returns will be associated with "out-of- money" calls though it will attract higher risk.

Do not fall prey

- Assignment fret

Those who trade in covered calls should not fear being assigned because assignments may actually be profitable if your shares are called as soon as you are assigned. There is also no need to fret over early assignment because options that possess extrinsic value do not normally get an early assignment.

- Deception of "fat" premiums

You may be tempted to sell an option because of the high premium. This is a mistake! The "highness" of the premium may be caused by the effect of information asymmetry relating to earnings or ratings. There is usually a high risk attached to such high premiums.

- Value is of essence

Avoid selling low priced shares just because you still make "profit" by selling the calls. This will be another financial blunder. You need to have an overall view of your profit and loss account, incorporating both realized and unrealized profits.

Construction of a Covered Call

There are two options by which you can construct a covered call. The essence of a covered call is to trade covered options. You can either chose a long or short option, depending on the level of risk that is attached to each option.

Calculating covered call returns

There are two broad ways to calculate returns on covered calls: static or flat return and if-called return. Since it is difficult to know exactly what the trading results will be on covered calls, its returns are taken as flat or static return; that is, the share of the price will remain unchanged when the call expires. In calculating covered call flat returns, we need to make some basic assumptions:

- In the "in-the-money" (ITM) calls, the callwriter will   be assigned
- In "at-the-money" (ATM) calls, the writer will not be assigned
- In   "out-of-the-money" (OTM)   calls, the writer will   not   be assigned

On the other hand, to calculate the return in the called return method, we assume that the call writer is assigned in the three situations (ITM, ATM, and OTM)

Now, let us see how we calculate covered call returns under these two methods.

Calculating return using a flat return method

The general formula for calculating a flat return on covered return is stated as:

R = TVP/NTD

where:

R = Return on covered call TVP = Time value premium

NTD = Net trade debit (also called break-even)

Please follow these steps to be able to get the variables above

(a)   Find the time value of the call, expressed as premium minus the intrinsic value

(b)   Calculate the net trade debit as stock prices minus total call premium

(c)   Divide (a) by (b)

For example, if the share of Unilever costs $22 and the $18 call sells at $5, Table 8.1 shows how the flat return is calculated.

Table 8.1: Calculation of flat return on Unilever share call

1   Premium $3.00

2   TVP   ($5 - $4) = $1

Note that $4   = $22   - $18 (intrinsic value)

3   NTD $22 - $5 = $17

4   Return $1/$17 = 5.88%

From Table 8.1, the flat return on above-covered call is 5.88%

Calculating return using if-called return

In this situation, the calls are exercised or assigned, and the formula for calculating the return is:

R = (TVP + PE)

NTD

Where

R = Return if called

TVP = Time value premium PE = Profit if exercised NTD = Net trade debit

The steps under this method are different from what   obtains under the flat return method:

(a)   Find the TVP and NTD as in the case of flat return

(b)   On "out-of-the-money" call, add extra profit derivable if the share is called, name it Y

(c)   Add Y and TVP, call it X

(d)   Divide X by NTD Example:

Suppose a Unilever share costing $20 with "out-of-the-money" call $21 is sold for $2. If the writer decides to call out the share at the $22 strike price, they will retain the $2 premium and still get an extra $1 profit, calculate return on the if-called. Table 8.2 contains this calculation.

Table 8.2: Calculation of if-called return on Unilever share call

1	Premium	$2.00
2	TVP	$2 (this call is time-invariant)
3	Extra profit if called $1($21-$20)	
4	Total profit	$2 + $1 = $3
5	NTD $20 - $2 = $18	
6	Return	$3/$18 = 16.67%

The return on Unilever shares if called is 16.67%

However, the above calculations are only applicable to expected returns or better potential returns because we can only know the actual return when the trade is concluded since it is difficult to predict events between the commencement of trade and its expiration with utmost accuracy.

Mutual fund: A rip-off?

Investing in mutual funds has become popular over the years, and many investors have not considered such investment as rip-offs. A writer defines business as "shrewd exploitation of the ignorant." Have you ever thought of what mutual fund managers do with your investment with them? They invest such funds, of course, and make fortunes. But you can invest your funds directly in the same opportunities as they do and make your own fortunes instead of the peanuts mutual fund managers give you. Would it not be better to be in control of your money now and in retirement? Yet, the expertise of mutual fund managers in investment cannot be overlooked.

Responsibilities of mutual fund managers

Business! That is what they do! Mutual fund managers are investment companies that buy shares and other financial securities with proceeds from the sale of shares in their fund to willing fund-holders/investors. Generally, mutual funds are open- end funds that are particularly attractive to small fund investors since most small fund owners will not be able to invest in shares directly.

Mutual fund managers technically create a feeling of security of resources in investors so that the latter will have a sense of safety of resources kept with the fund managers. Mutual fund managers pool the funds mobilized from several contributors together and plug it into highly profitable investments from which investors are paid marginal returns on their funds. Mutual fund management involves a complex and highly technical process in investing funds. Hence, the managers are specialists in speculation and investment in high-yielding securities.

Mutual funds: Good or bad

There are many advantages as well as disadvantages that are attached to mutual funds. We shall discuss some of these.

The good side of mutual funds

A mutual fund is a good diversifier because only one mutual fund can accommodate securities in their thousands. Considering the principle of large numbers, the mutual fund reduces default risks arising from company illiquidity or any other financial problem. To add to this is the expertise with which mutual fund managers manage their clients' funds. You need not be a financial expert in investing in a mutual fund as the managers are professionally trained to efficiently invest the funds at maximum returns.

Also, the fact that mutual fund is affordable makes it a delight to many public investing. Mutual funds can be purchased in bits or units such that it becomes easy for small savers to invest in it, especially because most mutual funds allow payment in installments. Furthermore, you can sell your mutual funds units or holding to generate cash to meet urgent financial needs. This feature makes mutual funds attractive to investors as it makes them liquid most of the time.

Another good feature of a mutual fund is its flexibility; that is, an investment can be switched among competing for investment alternatives such as capital market trading, money market, foreign exchange, calls, etc.

Mutual fund: A Caveat!

The good picture painted above does not rule out some problems that may crop up in mutual fund investment. As stated earlier, putting your money in mutual fund means that you entrust its management to independent managers whose degree of expertise determines your returns. If mutual funds managers fail to be more accurate in their projections, expectations, and judgment, your return will be adversely affected. This is why some see the mutual fund as "letting

another live your life." While we advise strongly that you watch the track record of mutual fund managers before buying their shares, we posit that not all their reports will be a true representative of the position of the fund in honoring obligations and enhancing returns.

Added to these are the occasional charges and fees placed on investors by the mutual fund. These charges and fees would automatically reduce your returns. The funny thing is that these charges are usually not part of the initial fund agreement but will be justified as your investment continues with the fund. To counter this problem, investors may wish to redeem their fund within a short time, but this also impairs their returns since the longer your investment stays with the fund, the higher it is expected to perform.

CHAPTER TEN

HOW TO SET UP A COVERED CALL PORTFOLIO

We have defined covered call in Chapter 8 as an options strategy that trades in an underlying stock plus an option contract at the same time. In most cases, the writer also owns the underlying stock but sells it as a call option for a corresponding amount or less than the stocks held and then watches until the option expires or is exercised. So how does one form a profitable covered call portfolio in the face of several options and choices available? This is the focus of this chapter

Creating a covered call: The steps

It is important to remind intending covered call writers that its main objective is to get returns through premiums on selling your own stocks. However, there are basic steps that are involved in creating covered calls

To create a typical covered call, please follow the following steps

- Buy/own a stock that is at least 100 units or a multiple of it. This is because covered calls are traded in 100 units.
- Then write/sell a call made of every 100 units of stocks owned by you. Every 100 units of stocks represent one (1) call contact, so if you have 1000 stocks, it means you can write or sell ten call contracts against the stock you own. This does not mean you cannot write fewer contracts, but it must be in 100s. The advantage of not writing all your stock is that in the event of the call being exercised, you will not forgo all your stocks. If you sell 700 stocks on a covered contract out of your 1000 units, for example, if the call is exercised, the 700 units will be called, but you still have 300 units that are left.

- Having written a call on the stocks you own; the next step is to wait and watch for the expiration or exercising of the call. At this waiting time, you are already better off because you have collected premium paid on the call at the onset. If the buyer does not exercise the call but holds it till it expires, the entire premium belongs to you. It is also possible that you buy back your call before it expires if the contract provides for that.

A covered call is a profitable investment that outstrips dividend payment. Selling a covered call means you are selling the right to buy your stock, but you are not necessarily selling the obligation to own the stock to them. Lyn Alden states that covered call buyers are "paying you for this option to increase their own flexibility, and you are getting paid to decrease your own flexibility."

But how do you know which stock to purchase in the first place? The following tips will help you select a good stock as well as maintain a

good covered call portfolio. These gems are termed the "four essential rules of selling covered calls" by Lawrence Meyers of the Wyatt Investment Research Centre. But we have split them into five here for clarity. They include:

- Track good stocks and go for them: You will need to do an effective tracking system that will help you to monitor stock prices over time in order to observe the trend of changes in prices. Technical analysis, such as the random walk strategy, can help. You can range-study stock prices. For example, stocks that have range-reflected behaviors will most probably be okay for selling against. In essence, since you will project ranges when stocks are undervalued, you can sell calls in order to generate income while you watch the market for favorable values.

- Do not sell your total position: This means you should still have a left-over or a buffer to own in case the stock rises above the strike price. The best way is to sell a part of your stock as a covered call and use the remaining as protection against unfavorable market swings.
- What is your goal? Your target return from the covered call must be defined from the onset. For example, you can target a return of between 2.5% return for a period of 30 days.
- Sell in bulk as much as possible: Selling bit-by-bit will whittle down your returns. Try to sell covered calls in bulk as much as possible.
- Volatility is key: It is always better to sell stocks that are not too volatile. Though a volatile stock can generate higher premiums, excessive volatility also has its own bad effect on returns

When to sell covered calls

Lyn Alden identifies three best times to sell covered calls, take a look at them below:

- When there is an overvaluation of stocks in the market, in which case the market has the likelihood of experiencing downtime for some time. At this time, a seller can make gains from two ends: options and dividends
- When there are stocks of slow growth firms such that a seller can at the same time get returns from capital appreciation, dividends and call premiums on the firms' stocks
- When one out of your stock is becoming overvalued in relation to its market price. A seller can make quick income by covered calls at strike prices that are greater than the actual value of the stock.

Risk versus return in covered calls

There are risks attached to covered calls chief of which result from being a holder of a stock position that its price can decrease. How much maximum risk can you bear in covered calls? It is when the price of the stock drops to zero, which is impossible. To calculate maximum loss one can get from a covered call, you only need to subtract the highest drop in stock price (0) from your entry price and add the premium you receive from the option to it. That is:

MLPS = (SEP-0) + ROP

Where

MLPS = maximum loss per stock SEP = stock entry price

ROP = received option premium

Example:

Suppose a seller sells a $10 stock and receives $0.50 premium, their maximum loss on the call is $10-$0.50 = $9.50.

On the return side, your maximum profit can be calculated as: You can only profit on the stock to the strike price of the option contracts you sold. Therefore, calculate your maximum profit as:

MP = (SP – SEP) + ROP

where

MP = maximum profit SEP = stock entry price

ROP = received option premium

This formula is premised on the position that a seller can only gain on a call, not more than the strike price of the covered call option. Figure 9.1 is a chart of risk/reward for covered call

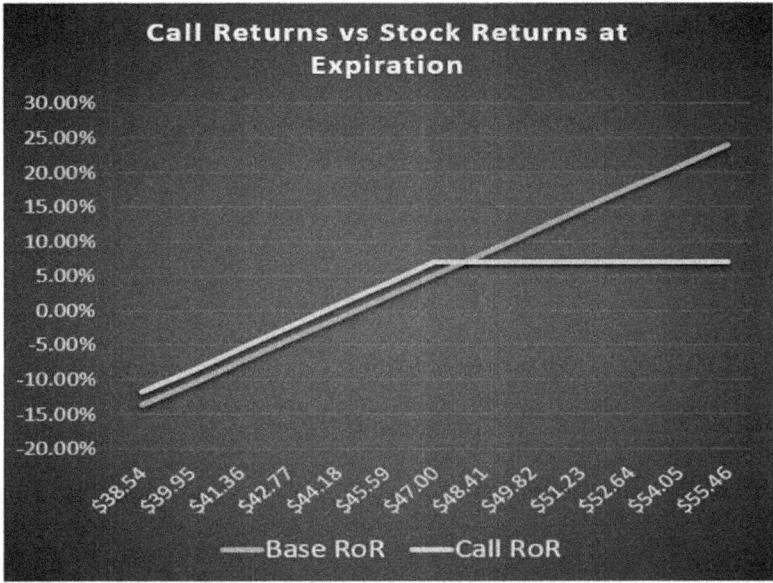

Figure 9.1: Call return vs. stock return at the expiration Adapted from Lyn Alden (2019)

The chart depicts that the call seller is capping their potential to

increase income by selling the call and exchanging this potential for any additional income and protection against downside.

Illustrating the construction of a sample a covered call

☐　　　　　Own at least 100 units of a particular stock. This is the same stock you wish to cover the call.

☐　　　　　You can only sell in ratio 1:1; that is, a call is 100 units of stock.

□   Try as much as possible not to sell all your stocks in a covered call.

□   Estimate your maximum profit, maximum loss potential and breakeven at expiration

□   Let's take an example:

Table 9.1 contains the construction of a covered call from an option chain:

The strike price ($) Call price ($)

The strike price ($)	Call price ($)
65	3.97
70	2.00
75	1.00
80	0.84

Suppose the market price of the stock was $65 when there were quotes for these options. The first thing a writer should construct a covered call is to own (purchase) 100 stocks at the trading price ($65) per unit of the stock. They then sell a call from the options in Table 9.1. Let's say they sell the second call ($80). We can then see their call position as follows:

Stock trading/purchase price = $65 Short call strike = $70

Premium = $2

Maximum profit possible = short call strike + premium − Stock trading/purchase price X 100

That is: ($70 + $2 - $65) x 100 = $700

Maximum loss possible = (Stock purchase price − premium) x 100, note that the stock price will go to zero at the expiration of the call

That is ($65 - $2) x100 = $6,300

Expiration breakeven price = Stock purchase price − premium = $65 - $2 = $63

Seller's position if call assigned: Suppose the call is assigned on short $70; this makes the seller obligated to sell 100 units of stock to the buyer at the given strike price, leaving the seller with a zero position though assignment gives maximum profit to covered call seller.

Probability of profit: over 50%

CHAPTER ELEVEN

BENEFITS OF VERTICALS IN OPTION TRADING

There are quite a number of benefits for option trading. Here we will be learning about some of them:

What is a vertical?

Verticals are a strategy in option trading where spreads are created with two different options expiring the same month but with different strike prices. They are verticals because the option prices and their expiry dates are listed vertically on the option sheet. In option trading, it is possible for investors, in their being speculative, to combine one or two calls or two puts: one bought and the other sold. When the two have the same expiry dates but different strike prices, the trade is said to have vertical spread.

On the other hand, a horizontal spread exists when the expiry date is different, but the strike price is the same. Furthermore, a situation where both the expiry dates and the strike prices of the two calls differ is called a diagonal spread. Our attention in this chapter will be on the vertical spread. Vertical trade is either bearish or bullish. While the bearish trade returns profit when stock prices fall, the bullish trade returns profit when stock prices increase.

Strategies for bullish vertical trades

In vertical trades, one can purchase an "In-the-money" (ITM) call and, at the same time, sell an "out-of-the-money" (PTM) call. For example, an investor can buy a call option at a strike price and a premium of and also sell another call on a strike price higher than the one they bought with the same premium but the market price of the stock at expiry rises; then they will exercise the option and make a profit. Another strategy will be to purchase an ITM call and sell another ITM call for a strike price greater than that which they purchased.

Suppose as the strike price is higher, the market price of the stock does not exhibit a sharp increase; the call will most probably not be exercised, so the premium belongs to the speculative investor. However, if the first call is exercised, the investor will get profit less the premium so that their overall profit will now be the return on the first call plus the premium on the second.

Strategies for bearish vertical trades

In a bearish vertical trade, an investor can buy a call at a strike price that is less than the market price of the stock and yet sell another call that has still lower strike price. A reduction in the market price of the stock when the call expires below the two strike prices means that none of the two calls will be exercised. However, when there is variation in the amount of premium so that the investor will receive a higher premium than the one they paid and they have a net gain.

Use of vertical spreads

So, what are vertical spreads used for? Two things: to reduce the payable premium and to minimize risks on options. These are called debit and credit spreads, respectively.

Debit spreads: Stock prices are highly volatile in behavior. When the stock price is highly volatile, the premium will be high and vice versa. Remember that a typical vertical spread sets a limit on your gain from an option, but it can also, to a large extent, reduce your cost when you place it side-by-side with a return that may accrue from a separate (stand-alone) put or call. So, in the event of high bubbles in prices, this type of spread can be used to offset volatility from one call to the other.

Credit spread: This spread considerably reduces the risk in written options. This is because writers face very high risk and collect the small premium, and an unfavorable option trade can completely neutralize the returns on good option trades. Someone sarcastically refers to option writers as "individuals who stoop to collect pennies on the railway track, and they happily do so until a train comes along and runs them over!"

Vertical spread: Choose right

You will now have to make a decision on which type of vertical spread you want to use.

A bull call spread: It is better to choose a bull call spread when rising bubbles make calls to be expensive, and there is an expectation of moderate return instead of massive profit. In a bullish market, moderate margins are expected when it is becoming obvious that stock prices are reaching the maximum point, and it is becoming difficult to garner higher gains. Again, you should choose a bull call spread when a stock exhibits considerable long-term gain potential but also has the probability of high bubbles/volatility caused by a drift in prices recently.

A bull put spread: You should try a bull put spread when you want to generate a premium on your way to slightly higher markets or decide to purchase stocks when prices fall and the market or to buy stocks at reduced prices when markets are jerky or changing. This is made possible due to the fact that a put (written) is exercisable and can be used to purchase stock at a given strike price. However, the credit received will cause a reduction in the cost of buying the stock different from when the stock was bought at the strike price. The advantage of a bull put spread is in its effectiveness in buying high- yielding stocks at low prices in situations where there are bubbles with an underlying trend in prices.

- A bear call spread: If you observe stock price is becoming highly volatile and that there might be a mild downside in returns, a bear call spread is suitable for you. In the peak of a bearish market or when stock prices are close to reaching a trough, there is high volatility caused by risk-averse and pessimistic dispositions of investors.
- A bear put spread: In cases where a moderate or considerable fall in stock prices or values with rising bubbles, it is good to go for a bear put spread. Also, you can opt for a bear put spread to reduce the payable premium.

The major determinants

There are salient factors to consider before you venture into your spread or options. Here are some of them:

Are you a bull or a bear? A bull is bullish, whereas a bear is bearish. Strongly bulls are, to a large extent, risk-averse and so it is better for them to go for a stand-alone call instead of a spread. You can also be a moderate bull who expects mild swings; then, you can go for a bull spread (call or put). For those who are mildly bearish and others who wish to reduce hedging costs for long positions, they can go for a bear spread (call or put).

Risk/return tradeoff: An option buyer will likely prefer lesser risk and high return than high risk while a seller or writer will likely prefer great risk and lower return

Volatility: When volatility is high, the option buyer will likely be at an advantage while falling volatility will probably favor an option seller. This is because while the buyer favors debit spread strategy, the seller favors a credit spread strategy

In summary, a moderately bullish trader will expect falling volatility, and okay with a risk-return tradeoff, you should go for a bull put spread. But if you happen to be modestly bearish, you expect rising volatility, and you want to limit your risk, you should go for a bear put spread.

Appropriate strike price

A general rule of thumb is to choose the deepest ITM call with a delta of not less than 90%, provided your resources can accommodate it. Alternatively, an investor can select the lowest strike price available in the market. This is because they want a call with the highest return (delta) as well as the price that is close to the stock price. But more importantly, the decision to choose a strike price is determined by the trader's outlook.

If, for example, the stock price of a bull call spread is expected to be

$60 till the expiration of the option, an investor can purchase a call at a strike price close to $60 and, at the same time, write a call at $65. If we assume that there may not be a drastic change in the stock price, the investor will not be willing to sell the call below $70 since they will receive a lesser premium on it. Notice that if they decide to buy a call for $63 strike price, it would be cheaper than when they buy a call for $60.

But there is a warning here. You need to evaluate what you are giving up or what you gain if you decide to accept other strike prices. The risks of getting a maximum return or that you will incur maximum loss must be well considered. Risks of returns or loss should form the basis of striking a price in the first place.

CHAPTER TWELVE

THE BEST GUIDE TO VERTICAL SPREAD

At the pool of having a good trade, one of the options for trading is having a vertical spread. There is a constant thing in trading; continuous change in the market situation. In the change in the market situation, the prices of things might either inflate or deflate depending on the situation. One other thing is that when there's likely to be a change, no one can predict.

Regardless of how expertise the trader is, the market informs no one of its volatile states. As people are trading, the input and output would begin to affect what happens next. Thus, it is safe for traders to actually buy some things when their prices decrease and sell when there is inflation. In short, a vertical spread is the option traders have to actually buy securities and sell at a higher price.

One of the things that makes a good trader is the ability to know when to buy and sell. To do this, it is important to the price of securities. The importance of prices cannot be overemphasized as they are the sole of trading. Price determines lots of things, and a good trader whose aim is to run at a profit would always think price is important.

In actuality, a vertical spread is a systematic strategy that would enable you to buy and sell multiple options at different prices. It is the strategy targeted at enabling the trader to know when to buy and sell using diverse options for a good profit. While checking through the vertical spread, traders would be presented with different options that have the same expiry date and undertone of security but different striking points and prices. By being of the same or equal chance of profit, it means that that they are of the same put and call. As such, being at the staking price level with very many options of when to sell or buy to safeguard profit would actually mean that the trader knows what exact profit or loss would be incurred for using the same security.

In trading, nobody wants to run at a loss even though some would still do what could amount to making a huge amount of profits; if there is no sacrifice, no one could be satisfied, profits of others. The question is, who would run at a loss? Knowing fully well that vertical spread involves the systematic writing or sales of the same puts or calls at different striking prices, it becomes pertinent to know the trending line at every given point in trading. Moreover, there are two basic options common with vertical spread; bull put spreads, and bull call spreads.

In both, the basic guide is to understand the point of cash flow and when to stake or strike price. This is because both work in the same way as the sole aim of spreading, but in the first place, what you need to do is to actually buy at a lower price and sell when the price inflates. With the idea of knowing the appropriate point for cash flow, traders must be careful to be sure of the market situation as everything could be vulnerable to lose within split seconds. In answering the question, you must understand how traders gain or lose while selling their options.

How Profits and Losses Work when Selling Verticals

In the long run, there are two things involved, in the vertical spread, debit, and credit. Although the aim of having or using vertical spread is to safeguard the trader and ensure smooth trading.

Having to sell verticals require adequate and more attention. The truth of it is that selling while trading could be riskier than buying. To sell, you have to know that you would be debited. Thus, if you wouldn't make additional high profits, it would be more grievous if you didn't get the amount you bargained in price.

In other words, you must position your strategies in such a way that it would enable you to know not only the profits that would be incurred for selling verticals but crucially the loss too. The following are ways in which profit and loss work in selling verticals (note that you have bought at some point, credited, before considering selling, debit):

Collection of premium

Being faced with diverse options is an indication that everything wouldn't have the same weight of safety. As such, it is crucial that one makes the right option, which could be time-bound. The same is applicable here, as there is a way you could buy and retain until the expiry date. The goal is to maintain the premium option till the expiry date elapse when you strike in order to make gain from higher prices. In other words, you would buy security and calculate the time of its expiration when the price would have increased. This is actually when you make a profit.

On the other hand, a loss could set in here when there is a kind of miscalculation of expiry. Another thing that could happen is the planned premium might not be worth waiting for its expiration in that the price could be stagnant. Even, it could be that the price of the options that could have given the premium was hit by an unforeseen circumstance. Most times, the best thing to do is to make sure all

strategies are up to the task and test of time so that when things boomerang, there will not be much loss incurred. Better still, it would be easier to manage the loss.

Acquiring high options

A good way for profit to work while making sales is to actually buy some expensive options. Before you buy this, it is important that you must have bought an option that has reduced in price and could be sold at that time. If this is done, you would then acquire expensive options and sell the cheap ones. The spreads would come into play in as much as the underlying security works in the direction of the planning.

Another thing to keep in mind is that the option to be sold must be expired before the acquisition of the expensive one. Remember, the profit would be moving smoothly in as much as the selling price is lower than the acquisition. Therefore, it is expected that the targeted options have the same value as it used to before expiry so that it could level up with other traders in order to ensure spread. If all these work well, then profit is guaranteed while selling verticals.

Contrariwise, a loss could set in when there's a kind of devaluation in the option that was supposed to be sold. This could be because the expiry date is yet to be grounded before selling, or it has exceeded too much that the options couldn't spread. Another thing that could happen might be that the options to be sold didn't go through at the appropriate time. It is important to note that the basic purpose of buying high and selling low is that the verticals could spread.

Thus, it behooves the trader to keep a keen eye on the strategies and make good calculations of the expected outcomes of the spreading and the trading, generally. There is a profit where there is loss; the ability to manage both guarantees much trading.

Having known some ways in which profit and loss work while selling verticals, it is important that you know what options there are to sell. With good knowledge of these options, compared, it would be easier

for you to make appropriate strategies that would not only work for a given period but also transcend both profit and loss. To manage good sales is to know the available options for sales with different prices. This would indicate good ways of making the right choices. Below are some of these options compared:

Selling Naked Call Options Compared to Selling Call Verticals

There are different strategies employed while trading. This is because of the nature of the market at large. This section focuses on "Naked call options and call verticals."

Selling a naked call option requires that the speculator make a sale of a security that isn't his or hers. In other words, the call is naked because the speculator has no power or control over it. Although being live on the market is risky, one of the riskiest tasks any trader would ever venture in is to sell a naked call. This is because the price could change at any point, which could even be greater than what was staked to buy.

Additionally, the buyer has the right to actually buy from different shares. Thus, sellers wouldn't want to keep losing them to the fate of not having stock. What happens in a naked call is that the seller would buy at the open market and make sure it hits the time-bound of the buyers in order to strike price. With selling at a good strike price, the sellers could be protected from running into an unprotected loss that would be huge and uncontrolled. In short, to sell a naked call option is to actually write or trade with one that doesn't have its ownership.

On the other hand, selling a call vertical only requires that the speculator buy at some point and sell when the one bought has expired. Thus, in this kind of call, the seller actually has the ownership of the stock.

Sometimes, it could be that the seller buys something at a lower price with the aim of selling at a higher price. Whatever the case, the strike price is in control as the seller has the right to the stock.

In selling the one that has expired, it could be that the one acquired more. Therefore, it would serve more like an upgrade, though one could run at a loss if there is no proper planning of the strike price runs at a deficit.

In conclusion, selling naked call options require that the seller has no ownership of the stock as the speculator hit the strike price while selling vertical call sellers would only need to make sure there is a time they have bought at a lower price and the time they are selling at a higher price.

Selling Naked Puts Compared to Selling Put Verticals

In selling naked puts, the seller doesn't have the ownership of the underlying proposition but only put premium price with the hope that the stock wouldn't rise too much in the long run. The underlying equity is what the seller always hopes will remain considerably stable as the buyer make deals. In the real sense, the seller would be on the lookout for a form of a decrease in the equity till the expiration. When the stock expires, the money gained would be from the decrease in underlying equity and strike price.

Conversely, selling a put vertical would involve the ability of the writer to have enough equity that would be sold at some prices higher than the purchases. In other words, the seller has control of the under equity and does not just wait for a decrease in the price of the underlying equity to make a profit. What happens is that the seller has two options; buying at a high price in order to sell stock that has lower prices or buying at a lower price and waiting for the premium time to make sales at high prices.

"Shorting" or Selling Put Verticals

The process of shorting a put vertical is when there is a kind of equilibrium short and long put at the different strike prices. The expiration period where both buyer and seller know their price is also at the same strike price.

The act of shorting or selling put verticals is simply ensuring that the expiration and strike price are equal while making sales, either long or short. Everything would respond as short with strike price being on the running scale margin of the expiration of the stock.

Illustration of a short put vertical

With less obligation, an investor could sell stock when there is a long and short put equilibrium but a different strike price. The price of selling would jointly be determined by the buyer and investor. To say, the investor would buy stock and keep it till there's a positive difference in strike price (price to sell) and the actual purchased price.

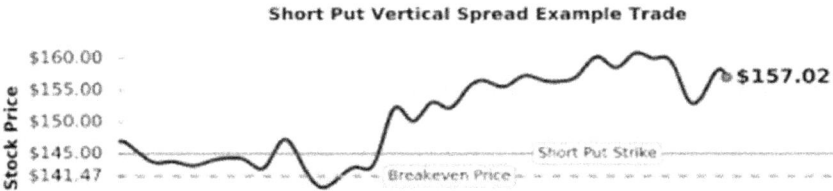

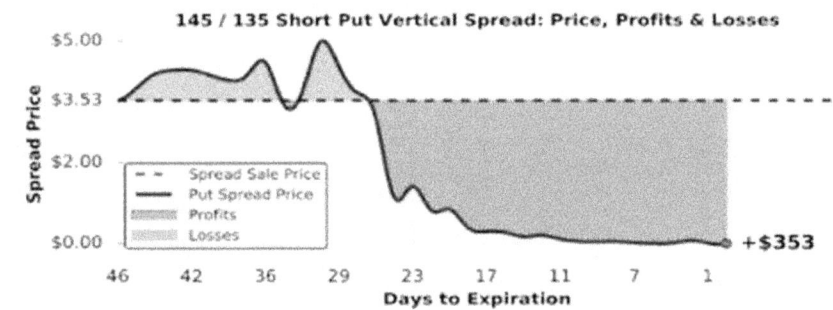

Short Put Vertical Spread Example Trade

145 / 135 Short Put Vertical Spread: Price, Profits & Losses

With equality, it signals the time to sell. Sometimes, the market situation could be that the strike price isn't perfect. But sometimes, it could be that investors would sell in as they would buy, especially when the strike price is considerably good.

This chapter has successfully explained what vertical spread is all about. This is done along the line of making a comparison of the types of options of making good verticals. Additionally, the times of profit and loss, together with how they work in the vertical

spread was dealt with. It is important you inculcate this in your trading scheme!

CHAPTER THIRTEEN

THE STRATEGY OF IRON CONDOR

"The temptation with condors is to wait that one extra day or week to squeeze out even more profit."

- **Michael Benklifa**

An iron condor in the stock market is a strategy created to take advantage of low volatility. The strategy of iron condor consists of four options, and each of these options consists of two puts, which are usually long and short, and two calls that are also long and short, and four strike prices, all with an equivalent expiration date.

Have you ever wondered why brokers or stock buyers have to make use of this strategy? The goal is to take advantage of low volatility within the underlying portfolio, stock, and asset of an individual or company. In saner climes, the iron condor strategy earns the utmost profit when the underlying asset closes between the center strike prices at expiration.

The iron condor features a similar payoff as a daily condor spread but uses both calls and puts rather than only calls or only puts. Both the condor and, therefore, the iron condor are extensions of the butterfly spread and iron butterfly, respectively.

Additionally, an iron condor is usually a neutral strategy and profits the foremost when the underlying asset doesn't move much. Although the strategy is often constructed with a bullish bias. Basically, the iron condor consists of 4 options: a bought put further OTM and a sold put closer to the cash, and a bought call further OTM and a sold call closer to the cash.

The profit of the trade is capped at the premium received while the danger is additionally discovered between the sold and the bought call strikes, and also the bought and sold put strikes (less the premium received).

Not a lot of people understand how iron condor works, but it is simple to understand. In understanding the iron condor, you must recognize the risk attached to the strike options. Interestingly, the iron condor strategy has a limited downside and upside risk. Are you surprised at this limited risk?

Well, there is often time a limited risk because the wings, including low and high strike options, protect the iron condors against some significant and essential moves in whatever direction they may occur. As a result of this limited risk, the potential profit rate of an iron condor is additionally limited.

The commission is often a notable factor here, as there are four options involved.

For this strategy, the trader ideally would really like all of the choices to expire worthlessly, which is merely possible if the underlying asset closes between the center two strike prices at expiration.

There'll likely be a fee to shut the trade if it's successful. If it's not successful, the loss remains limited. One way to consider an iron condor has an extended strangle inside a bigger, short strangle (or vice-versa).

Tips for constructing an iron condor properly

1.   Buy one out of the cash (OTM) put with a strike price below the present price of the underlying asset. The out of the cash put option will protect against a big downside move to the underlying asset.

2.   Sell one OTM or at the cash (ATM) put with a strike price closer to the current or actual price of the underlying stock.

3.   Sell at least one ATM or OTM call with a high strike price that is greater than the present price of the underlying stock, or market.

4.   Buy one OTM call with a high strike price that is greatly higher than the present price of the underlying asset.

The out of the cash call option will protect against a considerable downside move.

However, these options that are relatively out of the cash, called the wings, are both long positions. Because both of those options are further out of the cash, their premiums are less than the two written options, so there's a net credit to the account when placing the trade.

By selecting different strike prices, it's possible to form the strategy lean bullish or bearish. For instance, if both the center strike prices are above the present price of the underlying asset, the trader hopes for a little increase in its selling and buying price by expiration. Hitherto, it still has a lower risk and reward.

Iron Condor Profits and Losses

"Don't spend capital competing with people who are spending profits."

-       Moffat Machingura

You can experience profit and loss at almost every stage of stock trading and exchange, and it is essential that you understand how profit and loss in iron condor goes. The maximum or ultimate profit for an iron condor is that the amount of premium, or credit, received for creating the four-leg options position. The maximum loss is additionally capped. The utmost loss is the difference between the long call and short call strikes, or the long put and short put strikes.

Reduce the loss by internet credits received; on the other hand, add commissions to urge the entire loss for the trade.

The maximum loss occurs if the worth moves above the long call strike, which is usually higher than the sold strike, and sometimes, lesser than the long-put strike, which usually lesser than the price of a sold put strike.

A scenario of Iron Condor on a Stock;

Imagine that Amazon Inc. is going to be relatively flat in terms of price in the next two months; remember that you imagine this as an investor. Amazon Inc. Plan to implement an iron condor in their stock and business. Amazon's stock is currently trading at $212.26, and that is a good price. Right? The following will take place as they trade their stocks.

-        They will most likely sell a call with a $215 strike, and that provides them $7.63 as a maximum profit

-        They will buy a call strike of $220, and that will cost them $5.35.

-        The credit on the previous trade is $2.28 and $228 for one contract, which is the price of 100 shares. However, this is still incomplete, so in addition, a trader may sell a put with a

strike of $210. That sale will lead to a maximum profit of

$7.20, which will also give an opportunity to buy a put a strike of $205, which will cost $5.52.

-        Internet credit on these two sales in the previous point is

$1.68 or $168, that is, if you are trading one contract on each. At the end of the trade, the total credit for the whole trade is

$3.96 ($2.28 + $1.68), that is the addition of the credit from the previous trade, or $396.

This is often the utmost profit the trader can make.

This maximum profit occurs if all the choices expire worthless, which suggests the worth of the profit can be between

$210 and $215 when expiration occurs as imagined in two months' time. On the other hand, if the worth is above $215 or below $210, the trader could still make a reduced profit, but could also lose money.

The loss gets larger if the worth of Amazon stock approaches the upper call strike ($220) or the lower put strike ($205). the utmost loss occurs if the worth of the stock trades above $220 or below $205.

Assume the stock at expiration is $225. This is often above the upper call strike price, which suggests the trader is facing the utmost predictable loss. The sold call is losing $10 ($225 - $215) while the bought call is making $5 ($225 - $220). When thee puts expire. The trader loses $5, or $500 in total, for 100 share contracts, but they've also received $396 as maximum profit. At this rate, the loss is finally capped at $104, including the commissions.

Well, you may also assume the worth of Amazon dropped drastically, yet it did not drop not below the lower put threshold, it still falls to the range of $208. This will mean that the short call is losing

$2 ($208 - $210), or $200, while the long put expires nonetheless, which will lead to the expiration of the calls. On the other hand, the trader may lose $200 as a result of this trade yet receive premium credits worth $396 in premium credits. At this rate, they can still

make profits up to $196, with lesser commission costs, that is up to

$5000 deposit bonus

Trade forex and CFDs on stock indices, commodities, stocks, metals and energies with a licensed and controlled broker. For all clients who open their first real account, XM offers up to $5000 deposit bonus to check the XM products and services with no initial deposit needed. Learn more about how you'll trade over 1000 instruments on the XM MT4 and MT5 platforms from your PC and Mac or from the spread of mobile devices.

Trade Page Setup

"Trading effectively is about assessing probabilities, not certainties."

- Yvan Byeajee

Setup trading may be a sort of swing trading that's very fashionable today. Setup may be a particular configuration of trading price bars, usually with one or two other confirming conditions sort of a pattern or an indicator that delivers an expected outcome when there is a high sale of stocks. Most trade setups have catchy names; common names include pinball and coiled spring.

Each setup identifies a selected market condition that will be explained in layman terms of market psychology. One advantage of setup trading is that you simply are often out of the market until you notice a setup situation. You're taking no risk when you're out of the market.

Starting off early

"You never know what kind of setup market will present to you; your objective should be to find an opportunity where risk-reward ratio is best."

- Jaymin Shah

Irrespective of the kind of setup you have, setup identifies the possible conditions that may precede and accompany a change in price, supplying you with a start in entering a trade. Once you correctly identify the setup, the worth goes in your direction immediately. And when a robust move begins, the primary few days can account for 25 percent or more of the entire move. That's the thrust or impulse aspect of the latest move.

Effective entries are basically the hallmark of setup trading; however, risk management is the major feature of setup swing trading. So, it is appropriate for stock trading beginners. I will recommend that you must avoid handing over the profits of your stock by sitting-out retracement. Additionally, positivity   use   stops and   keep   traders updated.

Exiting the setup

For the foremost part, you don't scale into and out of setup trades. You identify the quantity to trade just one or two setups, you've got to watch an outsized universe of securities. If you specialize in steups to the exclusion of all the opposite concepts in technical analysis, you're at a loss for what to try to when setups don't appear.

To find your favorite setups, you've got to scan an inventory of securities. Amazingly, the best setups for you   may   appear insecurity that you simply wouldn't touch with a bargepole on a fundamental or value basis.

Setups require intense concentration and sometimes the power to trade actively during market hours. If you've got a day job, this task is often impossible to try to do. However, remember that active stop management is critical to your success. What does this mean? It basically means that you simply really should be out of the market altogether once you continue a business trip or vacation. The truth is war stories about some sour, hair-raising, and drastic losses usually involve not having placed a stop before making a trade and learning about some market-moving event only after arriving in an exotic location.

CHAPTER FORTEEN

UNDERSTANDING OPTION TRADING PROBABILITIES

When a trade is closed before it reaches its period of expiration and before it reaches max profit, the term "managing winners" is used to refer to it. There is a high tendency for traders to close winning trades when 50% profit is realized on traded capital.

Trade Page Profit and Loss. POP and Dealing with Winning Trades

Sometimes, however, traders may close winning trades with less than 50% profit realized, usually in cases where specific strategies such as calendar spread, diagonal spreads, and iron flies are used. For these strategies, the aim is to manage between 10 – 50%. There are a number of reasons for managing your winning when trading stock. They include the following.

Improving Win Percentage

It has been discovered that managing winning trades before they reach their period of expiration can experience an improvement in their probability of success. If you continuously enter trades with a profit probability of up to 70% but close them once you reach a certain profit percentage, different from the initial 70% target, you can increase your overall percentage of winning trades even higher than 70%.

This would happen because you're cutting off some risk, and also bringing about a reduction in time spent on the trade. You're making more money and saving your time.

Risk or Reward

A separate reason for which traders prefer to manage winning trades is the risk/reward shift that takes place when profits begin to come in. It is always a sad tale to see a trade that was climbing in profit begin to fall to a loss because you did not know when to take your profit and call it a trade.

For instance, in the case when you're selling a car for 2 dollars, with the maximum profit that you stood to realize on this car sale being 2 dollars, and with losses undefined. After ten days and implied volatility contracts kick in, which results in the option of being worth 1 dollar by now.

Since your maximum profit is the credit received for the trade, you have to reevaluate the risk/reward probability. Given the current position of this trade, you can only make 1 dollar more, while you still hold all the risk of the position, not to mention the fact that you could also lose the yet unrealized gains of the trade visible in the open position.

As the maximum profit draws even closer, your risk also begins to outweigh the potential reward of keeping the position open. The target of managing winning trades at about 50% is usually a good place for most trades in terms of curbing the risk/reward shift.

Lesser Trading Time

The major benefit of spending lesser time in trades is the fact that you can maintain the option to redeploy capital elsewhere in a new trade, which provides a higher chance of collecting more profit.

Using the example above, rather than waiting until the expiration period before hoping to make the extra 1 dollar profit, you could take the trade-off and look for a different underlying trade, which will provide you the option of collecting even more than that. This aspect of managing your winning trades can help you to improve your profit/loss odds each on a daily basis, and in the long term as well.

There are not many disadvantages to managing your winning trades early. However, a major point to bear in mind is the commission cost that you stand to run. It would be wise to ensure that you are covering commissions and not managing your winning trades earlier than you should. It would be sad to close a trade for winning 10 cents when that would likely inhibit your ability to pay commissions and still have a profit.

Break-Even Price Mean

Your break-even price is the amount of money, or change in value, for which an asset must be sold in order to cover the cost that has been accrued to acquire and own it in the first place. This term may also be used in referring to the amount of money for which a product or service must be sold in order for the manufacturer to cover the cost accrued in manufacturing it. In options trading terms, your break-even price is the stock price at which investors may choose to close the trade without running at a loss.

The concept of break-even prices can be applied to virtually any transaction. For instance, the break-even price of a piece of real estate would be the price at which the owner could cover the purchase price of the house.

Also, it is the interest paid on the mortgage, property taxes, hazard insurance, improvements and maintenance, real estate sales commission, and closing costs. If this amount is realized, the owner of the house will not get a profit out of it; nonetheless, there would be no loss incurred.

In managerial economics, the break-even price is also used to determine the costs of scaling the manufacturing capabilities of a product. Usually, when there is an increase in product manufacturing volumes, it brings about a decrease in break-even prices. This is because costs are spread over a larger product quantity.

The Break-Even Price Formula

The break-even price, in mathematical terms, is the amount of monetary receipts that match the monetary contributions that have been made. When sales match costs of production, the related transaction is said to be break-even. It sustains no losses and earns not profit in the process either. In order to derive the break-even price, you simply use the amount of the total service or assets rendered or trade a financial instrument with breaking even as a goal. For instance, the break-even price for selling a product would

be the sum of the unit's fixed cost and variable cost, which have been accrued in the making of the product.

In the case of an options contract, which could be a call or a put, the break-even price is the level in the underlying security that fully covers the cost of the option. It could also be called the break-even point (BEP), and it can be represented using the following formulas for a call or put option, respectively:

BEPcall = strike price + premium paid; BEPput = strike price - premium paid. Important notes

In manufacturing terms, the break-even price means the price at which the cost of manufacturing a product is equal to its sale price. In an options contract, the break-even price means the level in underlying security when it covers an option's cost.

The concept of break-even pricing is often utilized as a competitive strategy in order to gain market share.

Adopting the break-even price strategy can lead to the perception that a product is of low quality.

Break-Even Price Strategy

Adopting the break-even price is a common business strategy, especially for new commercial ventures. This is mostly common when a product or service is yet to be highly differentiated from those of the competitors present in the market.

Therefore, offering a break-even price, which is relatively low, without any margin markup, a business stands a chance to get a better share of the market, even though this is usually done at the cost of making any profit at all.

For a business to lead in cost by offering a break-even price, it would need to have the financial resources required to sustain periods

without earnings. After establishing market dominance, however, a business may begin to raise prices when weaker competitors can no longer contest its higher prices.

The following formula is used in calculating the break-even point of a firm

Fixed Costs / (Price - Variable Costs) = Break-Even Point in Units

The break-even point equals the total fixed costs, which is then divided by the difference between the unit price and variable costs incurred.

Break-Even Price Effects

Transacting at break-even prices has both positive and negative effects on the trader. Besides gaining market shares and fending off existing competitors, trading at break-even price is also useful in setting up the entry ante for new competitors in the market. This eventually leads to a controlling market position due to reduced competition.

A product or service's comparably low price, nonetheless, may create the perception that the products or service being offered or rendered may be of inferior value, thereby posing an obstacle to raising prices at a later time. In the case of others engaging in price competition, it would not suffice to price at break-even rate as this would not be enough to gain control of the market. In such a situation, losses can be incurred when break-even pricing births even lower pricing.

An Example of Break-Even Pricing

A firm, ABC manufactures widgets. The total costs of producing a widget per unit can be interpreted as follows:

| Physical Labor | $5 |
| Materials Used | $2 |

| Manufacturing Process | $3 |

Thus, the break-even price to recover costs for ABC is $10 per widget.

Now let's say firm ABC gets ambitious and becomes interested in making 10,000 such widgets. To make this happen, it will have to scale its operations and make significant capital investments in factories and labor. The firm, therefore, invests $200,000 in fixed costs, including building a factory and buying machines to be used in manufacturing.

The break-even price for each widget can be thus calculated:

(Fixed costs) / (Number of manufactured units) + Price per unit

i.e., $200,000/10,000 + 10 = 30$.

Thus, the break-even price for the company to manufacture the targeted 10,000 widgets is $30. The break-even price for manufacturing 20,000 widgets is $20 using the same formula.

Break-Even Price for an Options Contract

In the case of a call option with a strike price of $100 and an initial cost of $2.50, the stock's break-even target would be $102.50; anything in excess of that level would be recorded as pure profit.

Keynotes for sustainable success in option trading

A major benefit of options trading is that there are several ways to trade. Nonetheless, as mentioned in chapter three, the traders who enter the market with the requisite skillset usually outclass the ones who come in with only cash to invest and hopes of striking the right keys. A part of the required skillset in trading options is controlling your emotions. If you can do this, and you have time to trade during the day, you can choose either to be a momentum trader or a day trader.

If you would like to open a trade and then sell it a few weeks or days later for a better price, you can choose to swing trade options. If you are mathematical and would like to open a position for fixed, predictable earnings, then you should like to learn more about position trading.

The major ways to trade options are Day trading, Momentum trading, Swing Trading, and Position Trading. The process of deciding what methodology to pursue is dependent on your preferences and the time that you are willing to commit to trading.

Understand the Chosen Strategy

There are many ways in which you can profit from the day, swing, and position trading options. These various strategies range from simple to complex. You will only need to understand the approach that you choose to take. A proper understanding of a trading approach will include the maximum loss and profit, as well as the conditions under which they occur. Understanding options strategies go beyond mastering the calculations.

Choose the Right Stock

Every option strategy makes a profit only when the underlying stock has performed in a given way, and losses are made when the stock does not perform as expected or predicted. Therefore, irrespective of the trading strategy that you choose, you should pick stocks that perform in that very way. Hence, excellent technical and fundamental analysis skills are crucial to achieving success in options trading. Technical analysis is a vital tool in options trading as a means of accurate entry, and exit points are fundamental.

Allowing your winnings to run is one of the most effective methods for managing your winning trades in stock trading, although it is not the only one. You do not have to do it this way. On the other hand, the goal is to ensure that your winning trades pay you more than you lose on your losing trades. This means that on each trade, you must see that your risk ratio is lower than the expected gain on your trades. This is how trade is made successfully.

Allowing your winning trades to run is trading advice that we often hear in the stock markets. However, you must understand the difference between a trade and a long-term investment. If you aim at building a stock market portfolio for yourself, using a long-term investment perspective, then you should let your winning trades run.

The notion of stock portfolio diversification thus becomes extremely important. You can build a wallet and then hardly touch it so that it accumulates. Beginning traders often make the mistake of wanting, too quickly, to take their winnings on their winning positions, once they start to trend positively. It is also important that you learn how to identify and ride a positive trend for optimum profit, without getting greedy and emotional, so as to begin a profit/loss gamble by not taking your profits early enough.

Should you choose to trade short, medium, or long term, then it is a different matter. You have two options:

-       To let your winnings run

-       Or set yourself a price objective

If you set a price objective, you should place a take profit order and see that you do not have it moved. This way, your trade position is automatically closed once your objective is reached and your profit is pulled out to forestall a risk/reward scenario from playing out, to the loss of profits accrued.

CHAPTER FIFTEEN

FUNDAMENTAL ANALYSIS

What is Fundamental Analysis?

The term fundamental analysis (FA) is a method of measuring the intrinsic value of a security or investment prospect by examining related economic and financial factors. Fundamental analysts make investment decisions by studying any variable that is likely to affect the value of the security that they are considering for investment. These range from macroeconomic factors such as the state of the economy and the conditions of the industry to which the security belongs to microeconomic factors such as the effectiveness of the company's management and fiscal operations.

By now, you are aware of the importance of the connection between understanding the rudiments of running a successful business and making astute investment choices. Fundamental analysts basically check that the business behind an investment option possesses the viability to yield the desired profit.

The aim of fundamental analysis is to ensure that an investor can compare with a security's current price so as to ascertain whether the safety is undervalued or overvalued.

Fundamental analysis is usually considered to be in contrast with technical analysis, which forecasts the direction that the stock market prices are likely to take through an analysis of historical market data such as price and volume.

Top tools for fundamental analysis

To make any sense of the stock market and earnings, you will need to incorporate an understanding of certain terminologies known as fundamental analysis tools so that you can begin creating a picture of how much value the stock possesses. You should bear in mind, though, that some of the most well-known tools of fundamental

analysis are centered on values, earnings, and growth in the market. Here are some of the factors that you should recognize:

Earnings per share (EPS): You may not be able to learn much about a company from earnings or the number of shares offered or owned by you. However, when combined, what you get is one of the most commonly used ratios for company analysis. The EPS tells you how much of a company's profit is assigned to each share of stock. The EPS is calculated as net income, after dividends on preferred stock, divided by the number of outstanding shares.

Price-to-earnings ratio (P/E): This ratio is a comparison of the current sales price of a company's stock to its per-share earnings.

Projected earnings growth (PEG): The PEG is an anticipation mechanism of the one-year earnings growth rate of the stock.

Price-to-sales ratio (P/S): The price-to-sales ratio is the valuation of a company's stock price as compared to its revenues. It's also referred to as PSR, revenue multiple, or sales multiple.

Price-to-book ratio (P/B): This is also known as the price-to-equity ratio, which is the comparison between a stock's book value and its market value. It can be derived by dividing the stock's most recent closing price by the last quarter's book value per share. The book value of an asset is the value of the asset, as seen in the company's books. It is equal to the cost of each asset, less cumulative depreciation.

Dividend payout ratio: This is a comparison of dividends that are paid to the stockholders to the company's total net income. It helps to account for retained earnings, that is, income that is not paid out, but rather, retained for potential growth.

Dividend yield: This is also a ratio of yearly dividends compared to share price. It is also known as a percentage. Section dividend payments per share in a year by the value of a share.

Return on equity: To arrive at this, you'll have to divide the company's net income by shareholders' equity. It's also known as the company's return on net worth.

What is Technical Analysis?

Technical analysis is a trading method used to evaluate investments and identify trading opportunities by analyzing statistical trends gathered from trading activity. These include price movement and volume.

Different from fundamental analysis, which aims to evaluate a security's value based on business operations, including sales and earnings, technical analysis tools are focused on studying the price and volume. Technical analysis tools are used to examine the ways in which supply and demand for security will have an effect on changes in price, volume, and implied volatility.

Therefore, technical analysis is often used to generate short-term trading signals across various charting tools, yet it can also help to improve the evaluation of a security's strength or weakness in relation to the broader market, or to one of its sectors. This information helps analysts to improve their total valuation estimate.

The knowledge of technical analysis can be used on any security that possesses historical trading data. This includes stocks, commodities, futures, fixed-income, currencies, as well as other securities.

The Underlying Assumptions of Technical Analysis

In a series of editorials released by Charles Dow, he discusses the technical analysis theory. His theory includes two basic assumptions that have continued to form the framework for technical analysis in trading.

1.   Markets are made functional with values that represent factors influencing a security's price.

2.   But, even random market price movements seem to move in identifiable patterns and trends that tend to be repeated over time.

Dow's work forms the premise of the field of technical analysis today. Professional analysts agree on three general assumptions for the field of technical analysis. They are:

1: The market discounts everything

It is believed that among technical analysts, everything from the intrinsic operations of a company to broad market factors to market/consumer behavior has already been considered in the pricing of the stock. This point of view aligns with the Efficient Markets Hypothesis (EMH), which assumes a similar conclusion about prices. The only thing that remains is the analysis of price movements, which technical analysts view as the result of supply and demand, particularly to stock in the market.

2: Prices move in trends

Traders using technical analysts forecast that prices will experience trends irrespective of the time frame being observed, even in random market movements.

This means that a stock price is more likely to continue with a past trend than to break the trend. To a large extent, technical trading strategies are based on this point of view.

3: History tends to repeat itself

Technical analysts hold that history tends to repeat itself. The repetitive nature of movements of prices is often attributed to market psychology, which tends to be quite predictable, based on emotions like fear or excitement. Technical analysis makes use of patterns represented in charts to analyze these market movements, forecasting likely future market movements. While many systems of technical analysis have been utilized for over a century, they are still held as relevant because they illustrate patterns in price movements that often reoccur.

What are the Greeks?

The term "Greeks" is used in the options market to describe the different ramifications of risk that are involved in assuming an options position. These variables are known as Greeks because they emanate from Greek symbols. Each risk variable is borne out of the absolute assumption of the option with another underlying variable. Traders make use of different Greek values, such as theta, delta, among others, in order to assess options risk and for management of option portfolios.

The Basics of the Greeks

The scope of the Greeks encompasses many variables. These include delta, theta, gamma, vega, and rho, among others. Each Greek variable had a number associated with it, and that number tells traders something about how the option moves or the risk that is associated with that option. The essential Greeks (Vega, Delta, Gamma Theta, and Rho) are each calculated as the first partial derivative of the options pricing model.

Below are a number of the main Greeks that traders examine.

Delta

Delta (Δ) represents the rate of change that exists between the option's price and a $1 change in the price of the underlying asset. In other words, the price sensitivity of the stock option is relative to the underlying asset in question. The Delta of a call option ranges

between 0 and 1, while the delta for put option has a range between 0 and -1.

For options traders, delta also stands for the hedge ratio for creating a delta-neutral position. A less common application of an option's delta is its current probability that it will expire in-the-money.

Theta

Theta (Θ) is used to represent the rate of change that exists between the option price and time or time sensitivity. It is also sometimes referred to as an option's time decay. Theta is used to indicate the degree to which an option's price would decrease as the time to expiration decreases, given that other variables are kept equal.

Theta sees increase when options are at-the-money and decreases when options are in- and out of the money. Options that range closer to expiration also have accelerating time decay. Long calls and long puts will typically have negative Theta; short calls and short puts will have positive Theta. When compared side by side, an instrument whose value is not eroded by time, such as a stock, would have zero Theta.

Gamma

Gamma (Γ) is a stock trading representation for the rate of change existing between an option's delta and the underlying asset's price. This is called second order (second-derivative) price sensitivity. Gamma indicates the amount that the delta would change, given a

$1 move in the underlying security.

For example, assume an investor is long by one call option on hypothetical stock ABC. The call option has a delta value of 0.50 and a gamma value of 0.10. As a result, if stock ABC increases or decreases by $1, the call option's delta would thus be increased or decreased by 0.10.

Gamma is used for determining the stability of an option's delta: higher gamma values are an indication that delta could experience dramatic changes as a result of even small movements in the price

of the underlying asset. Gamma is usually higher for options that are at-the-money, while it is lower for options that are in and out-of- the-money and increases in magnitude as the expiration period draws closer. Gamma values are generally smaller and further away from the date of expiration. Therefore, options that have longer expirations are not as sensitive to delta changes. As the expiration period approaches, gamma values are typically larger, as price changes make a larger impact on gamma.

Options traders may choose to not only hedge delta but also gamma, so as to be delta-gamma neutral. This means that as the underlying price moves, the delta variable will remain close to zero.

Vega

Vega (v) stands for the rate of change that exists between an option's value and the underlying asset's implied volatility. This refers to the option's sensitivity to volatility. Vega is an indication of the amount that an option's price changes given a 1% change in implied volatility.

Due to the fact that increased volatility usually means that the underlying instrument is more likely to see extreme values, a rise in volatility levels will inadvertently increase the value of an option. In contrast, a decrease in volatility will have a negative effect on the value of the stock option. Vega is at its maximum for at the money options that have a longer time before reaching expiration.

Rho

Rho (p) is the stock trading representation of the rate of change that exists between the value of an option and a 1% change in the interest rate. This serves as a measure of the sensitivity to the interest rate. For example, let's say a call option has a rho of 0.05 and a price of $1.25. If the interest rates rise by 1%, the value of the call option will increase to $1.30, all else being equal. The opposite applies for put options. Rho is greatest for at-the-money options that last longer before reaching their expiration period.

Minor Greeks

Some other Greeks, which are not discussed as often, are lambda, epsilon comma, vera, speed, color, zomma, and ultima.

The Greeks explained above are the second or third derivatives of the pricing model, and they are known to have effects on things such as the change in delta with a change in volatility and so on.

The use of these minor Greeks is on the rise in options trading strategies as it is easy for computer software to quickly compute and account for their complex, elusive risk factors.

CHAPTER SIXTEEN

MAKING A TRADE: THE CHECKLIST

"Remember that stocks are never too high for you to begin buying or too low to begin selling."

Jesse Livermore

Making a trade requires diverse processes, especially making a profitable one. In the process of making a trade, the phases are done from consciousness to unconsciousness. As such, accuracy actually premises on the trader's ability to have internalized – build in unconsciousness –the things needed for a successful trade.

One of the things you would need as a trader is a checklist. As expected, there are times traders wouldn't need to always be reminded of what their checklist is about because they have internalized them –taken it to their unconsciousness. In actual fact, this could be regarded as a show of expertise. Bear in mind that having a mental checklist could be either learned differently from other things required in the trade or done as part of the trade.

Beginners of trade are always at the mercy of checking and verifying what trading checklist is all about. Either you're a pro in what you do or a novice, there is a checklist for whatever trading they're making. It is pertinent to have in mind that this chapter wouldn't be particular about a given checklist. This is because different checklists are trade specific and, as such, require that one have a slot or template which traders would put the specific trade.

Apart from this, having a checklist is aimed at knowing the best steps that a trader has to take and the best trade to venture in at a given point in time. Therefore, this chapter would provide the definition of a checklist, give the difference between a checklist and trading plan, and the importance of having and using a checklist.

What is a Trading Checklist?

A trading checklist contains the strategic steps that would be useful for a given trade pattern at a given period of time. To say, a trading checklist has the step by step processes that would be needed not only to trade for a given market situation but to also trade skillfully and safely.

Although a checklist is trade-specific, it needs to keep on changing depending on the SWOT (Strengths, Weaknesses, Opportunities, and Threats) analysis for a market situation. By being market- specific, it simply means that there could be needs to actually keep changing or adjusting the steps to suit a given period. Based on the fact that strength, weakness, opportunity, and the threat of a given trade would always change relatively to the capital, time, demand, and other factors, it is important to know the checklist that would guide the trader through the trading plan is supposed to be adjusted to the trade goals and situation.

Additionally, a trading checklist is more like a tool that would serve as a trade workup for your trading plan. While using the checklist, traders would be able to corroborate their imagined processes with the plan for trade. It is like the workbook that traders would use when they are live with trading activities.

When things are getting tussled in the trading phases, or there is a kind of change in the market, a checklist would be used by the trader to know the exact point where adjustment is needed and how it would be implemented. It could be that without a good checklist, it might be quite taking to know or carry out good trade, regardless of how expertise the trader is.

Going further, a checklist could be used as a simplified form of the whole trading process or market size. This is because it could be used as the tiny or systematic plan of the big trade. In reducing the whole trade and trading process into steps, the target is usually what could be the best trade for that period. Trading requires cumulative processes that would be running simultaneously; it is important that traders have the minute knowledge of the bigger steps. This would

enhance the productivity and safety of the trade. This is exactly what a trading checklist is.

Amazingly, a checklist could be of mental status. In this case, the traders might not need to write down a systematic process, but rather making the trade depicts or requires having the checklist internalized in the trader. In other words, there is some trading process that actually requires that one use the checklist. Another means of having a mental configuration of a checklist is to have learned it over time. This means that there would be a trading plan which checklist would serve as its step by step that is different from the processes involved in the trading processes.

In having a proper understanding of a checklist, it is important to have a brief knowledge of a trading plan, the bigger picture. Remember that a checklist is more like a subset of another set, so it would be appropriate to have some knowledge of what the set is about; the trading plan. With this, traders would be able to know when to apply the checklist out of the trading plan. Besides, a checklist works alongside the trading plan from which it has been crafted.

Trading checklist and Trading Plan: a dichotomy

Having given an explanation on what a checklist is, we'll need to know what a trading plan is?

A trading plan is the totality of your strategies that would be used while trading in the market. When designing a trading plan, the focus is usually on the target market. Thus, what is happening in the market at a given period of time would determine what the trading plan would be. Although trading specific, a trading plan would consist of two different parts; the permanent and temporal strategies. The permanent strategy is those that would be important for trading to keep running. Temporal strategy, on the other hand, would be those strategies that are sensitive to change in the market situation. Most times, the checklist would be kind of strong on those temporal strategies but flexible with the permanent.

On the differences between the trading checklist and plan, one is dealing with the total map of the whole strategies for the market, trading plan. While the other is dealing with the bit-by-bit processes that would be needed to carry out the plan. In a way, the checklist is the total breakdown of the trading plan.

Also, the target of the checklist is to see that the strategies specified in the trading plan are adequately followed; the trading plan is targeted at having the accurate way of tackling the market in general. So, the trading plan is focusing on what would be used to get the best of the market size, regardless of any unforeseen circumstances, a checklist is used to get the best of the trading plan.

Again, a checklist is from a trading plan, while a trading plan is from the need and demands of the market. Thus, before a good plan could be erected, there must be a proper understanding of the market size and situation. The checklist requires only a proper understanding of the trading plan.

With the proper understanding of the checklist and trading plan, why should you consider having a trading checklist? There is different

importance of having, know about, and using a trading checklist. The next section below will explain the totality of trading checklist for either experts or leaners of trading for optimum trading experience.

Importance of Trading Checklist

It is important to note that having a good trading plan or even a checklist doesn't guarantee successful automatic trading. This means that having the knowledge of something doesn't guarantee the adequate application of the same; the checklist isn't an exception. Therefore, apart from having the knowledge of the checklist, consider proper implementation. Below are some reasons for having a checklist:

To Win Trades

With a good checklist, it is easier to know when there are potential threats that could waylay winning a trade. Although it isn't automatic, it guarantees that traders would win a target. Apart from the fact that proper consideration of the market was what served as input to the checklist, the breakdown of the strategies enhances the trading process, thereby making winning a trade very sure.

Also, a checklist ensures winning trades because it helps to reduce the risk of picking a trend of the market at the wrong time. This is done through the systematic and coordinating working of the step by step guide of the general trade. If you would want to have good assurance of winning your trade, consider working thoroughly on not only your trading but its checklist. Sometimes, good strategies that win could be predicted by a good checklist.

It helps to reduce Risk

Although a trade without risk is almost not in existence as to when a trade is actually playing with risk. A checklist helps traders to minimize their chance of being victims of unnecessary or avoidable risks. With a good checklist, you are sure that potential risk is already calculated through the strategies. One thing to note is that the risk of the market might not be obvious in the first phase of trading –it might not even be present –as such, being totally careful is needed.

Therefore, some measures need to be in place to safeguard both the trader and what happens to the market at large. The market is in consideration because whatever happens in it is actually determined by the traders.

In reducing risk in trading, a checklist could inform the traders the particular time to trade, and those trading could be dangerous. Regardless of the prowess of the trader, there are times that risk could be inevitable. Although this wouldn't guarantee that traders are free from risk, it only means that a checklist could help in calculating and managing it. With reduced risk, traders have enough assurance and confidence to actually trade with adequate success.

Reduce Emotion in Trading

In trading, there are lots of risks available, which could make the trader to be tensed. When traders are in a tense state, even the cheapest trade could be lost. This is the reason it's important to curtail risks and potential risks before they grip the trader. One of the ways to do this is to have a good checklist that could keep the trader on the right track at any point in time. When trading begins, there could be need to adjust the strategies in use, so going through what is in the checklist is essential.

With reduced risk, it is possible to trade using the checklist effectively. What would be standing in for the emotion is the breakdown of the guide for winning the trade- the checklist. It would be easier to trace the particular point of the problem when the breakdown is strategically slated. This is that once the trader could have the predicted plan from the checklist, having an increase in emotion because of fear of loss could be curtailed. A good checklist would boost the morale of the trader to see the possibility of winning trade all the time.

Building Good Discipline

When trading lives with things working smoothly, it is possible that you would want to alter the plan that has been slated without

considering the outcome. This is because traders are fond of increasing their chances of making an additional profit, so it causes potential loss most times. It is good to make a move for a good profit, even beyond what has been planned, having a good discipline mindset in order not to run at a great loss is key. When traders want to go over the board, a checklist could help to curtail them by showing how risky the step could be to the entire trade.

In being discipline, it might not be that the present step could lead to a loss. Rather, it could be that sequent steps could depend on it in order for trading to move smoothly. Besides, a sudden change in the strategies that have been properly used could be risky regardless of any benefit ahead. With a checklist, it is possible to make things within the plan in order to avoid loss. A good checklist would keep the trader on a good mindset of discipline. Most times, the trader would be exposed to the result of the trade using the steps within the checklist.

In conclusion, the need to have a checklist can't be overemphasized. As such, a good trader would want to have it close to them when they live on the trading market. Someone once said, if one fails to plan, one has planned to fail. Therefore, ensure you have a checklist for use. It is part of the heart of the trading. You wouldn't want to be without such that could help you reduce risk, increase productivity, reduce emotions, and build good discipline.

CHAPTER SEVENTEEN

STEPWISE ACTION FOR SUCCESSFUL TRADE-IN OPTIONS TRADING

Options are a specific type of derivatives agreements that allow one to purchase an underlying asset on or before a specific date. Derivative agreements are contracts that originate its worth from the performance of an underlying entity. With a derivative contract, one does not own the underlying asset, but an interrelated asset whose worth is affected by fluctuations in the rate. With an option contract, you have the right but not the duty, to buy or sell an asset at a prearranged price in the future.

A call option permits you to purchase an asset at a predestined date and predetermined value. A put option permits you to sell an asset at fixed prices and sell dates. An option is used for speculation or hedging, and they also offer high advantageous control, allowing you to sell big contracts and hypothetically make big money. And also, options trading has limited risk. To exploit these advantages efficiently, one has to put in concise and crystal-clear actions.

There are several strategies to engage in trade options; it is much more than just put or call options. Understanding these strategies would help you better manage your risk and seek new trading opportunities, thereby achieving successful option trading. Some other strategies include; covered call, married put, bull call spread, bear put spread among many others.

Covered call strategy is also referred to as buying the right strategy, and it involves the outright buying of stocks. The number of acquired shares should be equal to the number of call options contracts sold.

Married Put strategy works like an insurance policy against long term losses. It involves the downright procurement of stocks and at the same time purchasing put options for a corresponding number of shares or portions

The Bull Call strategy implies that one can buy call options with a specific strike price and simultaneously sell the same number of purchased call options at an increased strike price rate.

Bear Put Spread Strategy is similar to the Bull Call Strategy; however, differs because it involves the buying and selling of Put options. In this strategy, buying put options at a fixed strike price, they are sold at a decreased strike price.

Step-by-Step Action to Prepare for Trade

While you are starting, I recommend that you do the following

Make Your Market Prediction

Carry out the necessary research, underline any opportunity to make a trade, and determine how you are going to try and make a return. With Options, there are several different outlooks that you can profit from. You can partake in options trade where you can earn from an asset simply up-rising in price and also from an asset going down in price, but you can also profit from other scenarios. All you need to do is to take advantage of the right strategy, and you can buy and sell options profitably.

For example, if you have underlined an asset that you feel is going to be stable in the market price for a while, the right strategy would help you benefit from it. Or probably you have noticed an asset that fluctuates moderately; the right strategy is all you need to make a profit from any moderate move in either direction. There is always a strategy that you can use to make a profit from any Option situation.

So, if you are sure that you have successfully predicted what would happen to that asset, you should choose a strategy and go on with your investment.

Set Your Goals

What are your targets? What do you aim to achieve with this investment? It is not a necessary step, but it is good for you to set your investment goals. Your main concern should be on "how much profit do I wish to make?" if you do not make clear this knowledge, you might find it difficult to judge if your trade was successful or not. You should also set your time target; "within what timeframe do I want to make this amount of profit?" Setting targets would help you in taking the right steps in your trade.

Select a Suitable Strategy

The key to success in options trading is combining the right strategy at the right time. There are limitless ways that you can conglomerate various options positions to profit from your underlined asset. After you have predicted how you expect the price of an asset to move, you need to choose a tactic rightly founded on what your outlook is and the goals that you have fixed. We have discussed several strategies in options trading, so you might want to re-read that chapter. You should take note of these strategies so that you can use the appropriate one to try to make your intended profit from the market movements that you have predicted. These strategies can be simple or elaborate; you just need to understand them and choose their suitability for your intended trade. You should also, at this point, take risk management into mind. Consult your trading plan to know your risk level. Don't bother about mastering the strategies; the more you use them, the more they become relatively easy.

Choose Your Position

It is vital to do position sizing so that you can control your budget. Decide how much capital you want to risk. No matter your confidence, try as much as possible to limit the capital you would be investing in or putting in the trade. It is not just about how much money you are paying but about how much income you are putting at risk. Take your potential losses into contemplation; this eventually, is how much of your capital is at risk. This step requires utmost caution, care, and meticulousness as any mistake can lead to losses that will devastate your investment capital.

Plan Your Purchase

To enter the position and trade, you need to make the necessary order(s) with your broker. You should even deposit some funds with your broker ahead of time so that you can

place orders immediately. Wasting time transferring funds after the market is open can cause you to lose money or even the entire investment opportunity.

Plan to Sell

Planning to sell is planning to exit the option position as the expiration date approaches. Do you want your position to run on till expiration, or do you plan to close up sales early? A plan that when you make a particular amount, you will exit your option position. If you occupy multiple option positions, you should decide if you'd be exiting them simultaneously or one after the other. You can exit by monitoring the market or by setting up automatic stop points.

Steps to Help You during a Trade Action

There are six (6) steps in this piece that would help you get to buy and sell Options. Step 1-4 would help you establish a market predisposition (also called bias) and identity the Buy Put Option trade. While in addition to that, Step 5-6 would help you identify when to sell your Call Options.

Step 1 – Do not be in a hurry! Remember that the patient dog eats the fattest bone. Wait for 15 minutes after the stock market opens to create your market predisposition. You need to exercise patience and take a brief study and insight into the market. The most successful options trading strategies should not only focus on the price but should also take time to study various investors and the position in which they occupy. The stock market opening price is significant to note, usually the most vital price to note, but all things being equal, this is a case of look before you leap.

Step 2 – Ensure that your 15-minutes wait is optimistic and of rising value, because the aim is where the smart money is.

Step 3 – Check for the rising value to confirm that the Relative Strength Index (RSI) is above 50 levels. Since we want to make sure of the bullish price, i.e., rising value, make use of the RSI indicator for confirmation. Don't bother about the oversold or overbought market conditions. The market can stay longer in that way more than you can stay in credit.

Step 4 – Buy! Right at the opening of the second 15-minutes candle, purchase a call option. Since you already know that your smart money will be used for smart choices, don't waste any more time.

Step 5 – Choose a valid expiration cycle, the nearest one most preferably. Settling on the expiration date is also part of the fundamentals of a Call Options contract. And since you most likely would be selling your call option that same day, choose a weekly expiration cycle. Meaning that if it is a day trading, you should choose a weekly cycle.

Step 6 – The next step is to pay attention to the most critical aspect of options trading, which is profit. If you are not interested in owning those share stocks but just making a quick profit with your call option, you should know when to sell your call option and make a profit. Knowing when to make a profit is as important as knowing when to enter the trade. As soon as you witness two consecutive bearish (falling value) candles, sell.

Taken a journey to understand how to have successful trade options, you need to know how to choose the right option contract. Option trade contracts have some amount of risk; this is because options can be useless on their expiration date. There's no need to be anxious; however, take time to answer the following questions when selecting your options to help you manage your risks.

How long do you want to trade for? Day trading or long-term trading? If you want to trade for a short period, you should buy contracts that are quick selling.

How well can you tolerate risk? You have to understand your level of tolerating risk and take your steps carefully.

How volatile are each of the potential assets? Option contracts have a high level of implied volatility/instability. They experience substantial changes in value in the first 30 minutes of trading. It is noteworthy that high volatility implies higher risk and higher rewards

What are the past returns on the options contract? Study the history of the Options Contract that you are eyeing to know if it is a worthy venture of a failed enterprise.

When trading stocks, it is essential to take note of the market sentiments and how the big players have positioned themselves in the market so that you don't make a wrong investment that would, in turn, decimate and devastate your capital. I have discussed actions you can take to ensure that you will come out successfully in your options trading venture. For a beginner, these actions would help you and guide you on how fast or slow your actions should be to

help you meet your profit target and, of course, your time target till you get the hang of options trading and become a master of it. When you get the hang of it, you would be able to choose suitable strategies that would fit into other options choice.

Remember that a specific trading strategy might not seem best for options trading, so you'll need to combine two or more strategies. So that their principles and theories can help you achieve your desired effect and reach your specific goals and target. As long as you put all these steps we have discussed into practice, making a profit from options trading and becoming a Master of It will not be something difficult or impossible anymore.

CHAPTER EIGHTEEN MAKING A TRADE

"Trading on the share markets is an excellent way to increase your wealth and elevate your income levels."

- **Yogeshwar Vashisthta**

What do you do when you decide to go shopping or get some food at the grocery store downtown? You will most likely pen down all that you want to buy, just in case you are one of the most indecisive people. The fact that you have a shopping list is a good plan, and you will probably not miss any item, or forget to purchase any item.

Making a trade is likened to shopping, there are many items to shop, even though you have your credit card loaded with money. You may still walk out of a mall empty-handed because you never had a list. Thus, you found it challenging to make the right choice. Sometimes, Stock traders are faced with this kind of challenge, not because they are poor, but because making a trade can just be a daunting task.

In business and related matters, there is this old saying that if you fail to plan, then you have planned to fail. Of course, it may sound artfully persuasive, but it is true. People who are interested in being successful, traders inclusive, have to adhere strictly to those words because their success is grossly dependent on it. If we ask any trader who makes money regularly, it is most likely they will tell you that you have two choices, either to follow a laid down plan for success or failure systematically.

Perhaps, you've already written an investment or trading plan, congratulations, you're among the very few who do. Usually, it takes a lot of time, effort, and consistent research to develop an approach or system that works in the financial markets. I believe that if you successfully do these, you would have eliminated one major hindrance to a successful trade by crafting a well-detailed trading plan.

The significance of having a detailed trading plan for achieving success cannot be overemphasized. Although a trading plan should be written down and followed with some sort of rigidity, it should also be subject to consistent evaluation, and adjusted along with a dynamic market situation. When preparing a trading plan, the personal goals and style of the trader should be considered.

Just like with any other venture, one important factor to consider is timing; timing is important. It is the ability to know when to enter a trade or exit it. At times success could be slow if your plan uses techniques and methods that are not properly planned or prepared, but one thing you may be rest assured of is that you're at least in a position to modify your methods and see positive results. Also, when you document the process, you will be learning what works, and what doesn't, how to avoid the mistakes that new traders sometimes make.

Let us examine a few ideas to help you with the process of whether or not you have a plan in place yet or not.

"A peak performance trader is committed to being the best and doing whatever it takes to be the best. He feels responsible for whatever happens and thus can learn from mistakes. These people typically have a working business plan for trading because they treat trading as a business." – Van K. Tharp

Avoiding the pitfalls while you trade

Treating trade as a business is essential if you want to succeed at it. So just opening a brokerage account, buying a charting course and reading some books, and starting trade with real cash is not a business plan. To say what it is, it is set up for failure.

A trading plan should be appropriately written down with obvious signs that can't be easily changed while you are trading but should be subject to re-evaluation during times when the markets are not functional.

The plan may change with market conditions and possible government policies that may arise and might see some adjustments as the skill level of the trader gets better. Every trader would have to write their plan. The plan should be written according to the goals and personal trading styles of the trader. It is of no use trying to use someone else's plan, which does not reflect your trading features and patterns.

So, no two trading plans are the same because no two traders are entirely alike. Each trader's approach will depict pertinent factors such as risk tolerance and style of trading. Some other necessary components of a detailed trading plan that a trader should look at include the following:

1.   Assessing Your Skill/Trade.

Are you ready to trade? Have you gotten your system tested by trading it on paper? How much confidence do you have that it will work in a live trading environment? Can you follow your signals without having to halt your guts intermittently? Trading the markets is actually a duel between you and the real professionals out there. The professionals don't mind taking all the profits from the rest of the traders who do not have a solid plan, who make costly mistakes and sometimes lose a great deal of money.

2.   Mental Preparedness.

Another great way to get started is to be mentally prepared. How do you feel about the trade? Did you get enough rest? Do you feel you are up to the tasks upfront? If you discover that you are not psychologically or emotionally prepared to engage in the market warfare, you can take a few days off; else, you might end up losing a lot more than a few days. So, ensure you are not angry, or distracted from your task or preoccupied with some trivial issue. These things can have a significant impact on your success.

Most traders have a market slogan or phrase that they repeatedly say before the day begins to get them ready for that day. You could create one that gets you properly into the trading 'Spirits.' Besides, your trading zone should also be free of distractions. Remember that this is a business, and distractions could be costly.

3.   Set Your Risk Tolerance Level

Here you would have to consider your risk tolerance level. How much of your portfolio of assets should you risk on a single trade? The answer to that would depend on your trading style and the level of your risk tolerance. The level of risk may vary but could have a range of about one percent to five percent of your asset portfolio on a given day of trade. That means if you get to lose that amount at any point in the trading day, you would get out of the market and remain out. So, it is better to pause and take a break, then come back to wrestle another day.

4.   Set your goals

Before you enter into any form of trade, you need to set profit targets that are realistic and also set the ratio of risks to rewards. What is the lowest level of risk to reward you can accept?

Most traders will not enter into a trade, unless the potential reward is at least three times greater than the risk involved. For example, if your stop-loss is one dollar per share, your goal ought to be three dollars per share in profit. So, you should set your profit goals on a

weekly, monthly, and annual basis in dollars or as a percentage of your asset portfolio and have them reevaluated regularly.

5.   Do your assignment when the markets are closed.

When the markets are on a break, what do you do? Before the market re-opens, do you keep yourself abreast of what is going on in the stock market world? Are the foreign markets experiencing a boom or a decline? Are the index features of S and P 500 index up or down in the pre-market? You could use Index features to gauge the mood of the markets before the market re-opens because future contracts usually trade during the day and also at night.

You could also decide if you want to trade ahead of a very important report. For most traders, it is more advantageous to exercise patience until the report is released rather than taking risks and going ahead to trade during the phase of volatile reactions to reports. Experts' trade based on certain probabilities. They do not gamble. Going to trade ahead of an important trading report can be classified as gambling because it is not possible to know how the market will react later on.

6.   Set Rules for Exit.

Many traders usually make the mistake of concentrating almost all of their efforts on looking out for only buy signals but pay very little attention to when and where to exit the market. Most traders cannot sell if the markets are down because they do not want to accept a loss. But you would need to learn to accept losses, or you might likely not make it as a trader. If your stop gets a hit, it means you were not correct. So do not take it to heart. Most professional traders usually lose more trades than they win, but by properly managing money and limiting their losses, they still come up with profits.

So, before you enter any trade, you should know your exit points. About two possible exits are available for every trade. First, what's your stop loss if the trade does not go in your favor? You must have it written down. Having a mental stop is not usually feasible.

Second, every one of your trade should have a target profit, so that the moment you hit the target, you can sell a portion of your position and then move your stop loss on the rest of your position to the point where you are okay if you neither make profit nor loss.

7.   Leverage the computer in setting your entry rules effectively

It is important to note that exits are more important than entries. Your entry system should be complex enough to be effective, but also simple enough to facilitate quick judgments. If you have twenty conditions that must be achieved with most of them being subjective, you will find it really difficult or even impossible to make trades. Some studies have shown that computers actually make better traders than people because these devices do not have to think or feel good before making a trade. Every single decision is solely based on probabilities and not on emotions.

8.   Ensure your records are kept properly

Most successful and experienced traders are really excellent at keeping their records. Whenever they win a trade, they would want to know how and why they did. Also, they would still be interested in knowing the same if they lose, so that they won't have to repeat the same mistakes. You could write down details such as profit targets, the exit and entry of every trade, the time, resistance and support levels, opening range on a daily basis, market open and close for each day. You could also record a few comments about why you made such trade and also the lessons you learned from it.

Also, you should have your trading records saved so that you can go back and do some analysis to the loss or profit for a particular system, the drawdowns which represent the amount lost per trade using while a trading system, average time per trade which enables you to calculate the efficiency of trade, and other important factors. Do not forget that it is a business, and you are the main accountant. I'm sure you desire that your business thrive successfully.

9.   Analyze your performance

At the end of each day's trade, you should first get to understand the why and how behind every one of your trades. This is more important than trying to add up the profit or loss. After an analysis of your why and how, you should write down your conclusions in your trading journal so that you can always make reference to them later, drawing from the experiences when making future trade decisions. Do not forget that there'll always be some lost trade. So, your aim would be basically to craft a plan that makes gain over the long run.

Finally, successful trading practice does not guarantee that you will find success at the start of your trade. Sometimes, this may become aggravated when emotions set in. Successful trading gives the trader a certain level of confidence in the system they are using if the system generates good results in practice. Gaining enough dexterity to make trades without having to second-guess or doubt your decision is really important. Confidence is really paramount, and that's what the trading over time would build into you.

The only way to guarantee that a trade will make a profit is simply based on the trader's skill and broad knowledge of how the stock market system operates. So, sometimes you win, other times, you lose. Even the Pros in the trade know before they enter any trade that the odds are in their favor or else, they would not be there in the first place.

CHAPTER NINETEEN

SAVVY STEPS FOR SELECTING WINNERS

"It's far better to buy a wonderful company at a fair price than a fair company at a wonderful price"

– Warren Buffet

To start with, it is important for investors to know and understand the know-how of selecting winners before investing. Looking out for very important information is critical to your success in stock-investing. Starting your career or sustaining your career as a stock investor, you must be ready to engage in a deliberate and personal gathering of information about the kind of stock you are interested in.

Consequently, this simply means that you will have to run microeconomics; you look out for all the companies you can invest in and evaluate each of the company's products, services, and other factors that may influence your value. Why must you do that? It helps you determine whether or not a company is worth investing in or not. You want to know if they are strong or weak, healthy, or unhealthy. You want to know exactly where the company was, where they are, and what future plans they have for growth and income. In investing, keep in mind the fact that you must put your money into companies with the track record of a thriving industry.

From what Warren Buffet said above, it is clear that investing is not just compelled or initiated because a stock is cheap. Neither should it be because it is high. Investors must take to cognizance of the price before, and the value that will be added after an investment is made. Paying much for a less valuable stock is like throwing one's treasure into an ocean.

A very clear attention should be given to value-investing, paying a low price relative to the value you receive. Then, how do you, as an investor, select carefully, winners to invest in for great profitability? What are those things to give attention to before making an investment or making a huge commitment to a market or stock? Let's see steps to selecting your winners:

VALUATION

Valuation is the ability of the investor to adequately determine the profitability of a firm's stock before investing. When value-investing is mentioned, what is the first name that rings in your mind? Warrant Buffet, right? Or perhaps, Benjamin Graham. Warren buffet talking about the rule of investing said;

"Rule No 1 is never to lose money. No 2 never forgets the Rule No.

1."

In investing, every investor wants to buy a product as low as possible. Before investing your money, you must first decide on your capital; that should come first on your list. Also, many investors focus on the market instead of focusing on the stock. To make the most of your investment, you must focus more on the stock and not the market. Once you are certain of the credibility and valuation of a stock, you can go for it without paying too much attention to the broader market.

Think of it this way; you are bid by a seller to a bakery to buy bread. You love bread, and you are willing to purchase. In this example, take the bread as the companies, and the prices as the price to pay for the companies' stock. Now, the bakery is your stock market. After showing interest in buying bread, it happens that two brands of bread are similar, but one costs more than the other. Which will you possibly go for? The chances are that you'll judge both qualities, and if indeed both are similar, you take the cheaper one. What if the two brands are not the same in quality but the same in the price? You sure will go for the best quality. That is the whole idea of valuation. Nothing is as important as finding value for your investments.

In accessing a stock's value, you can use the following valuation ratio;

Price/ earnings ratio. Price/ sales ratio.

Price/ book ratio.

Price/ operating cash flow ratio.

Price/ earnings ratio:

The price/earnings ratio is one of the most used valuation measures. Earning and price refer to the gain or money earned by a company after paying its bills. The price-earnings ratio displays what the market is ready to pay for a stock based on its recent earnings. You should pay close attention to valuing a company based on its profit- making because having a share of stock in such companies automatically means you have a part in its profit. How do you then calculate the price/earnings ratio of a particular stock? First, you get the stock's share price and its earnings over the last four quarters, which is often called 12-month-trailing earnings. Then you can use the formula below to calculate the P/E ratio.

P/E ratio = Market value price per

share

Earnings per share

For example;

If a company's stock is currently trading at $100 a share and its earnings per share for the year is $10. The company's P/E would be calculated like this:

10 = $100

$10

The $10 there indicates the amount the investors are willing to pay.

Price/ sales ratio:

In comparing the value of stocks, investors use P/S ration in knowing a company's capital and revenue (sales) to determine the proper value of their stock. It is used to determine how much a company has at hand before taking expenditures into account. This ration can also be used to predict the future performance of a company.

Price/ book ratio:

P/B ratio is used by companies to compare and check the market capitalization and book value of a firm. It's calculated by dividing the firm's stock price per share by its book value per share.

Formula: Total assets- total liabilities/number of shares outstanding.

Price/ operating cash flow ratio:

This has been considered the best valuation ratio by many investors. Price/ operating cash flow ratio is a financial multiple which equates a firm or a company's market value to its operating cash flow. It shows the current amount of a company's stock relatives to the amount being generated by the company.

Formula: we can use two basic formulas for this valuation ration.

1.   Using the company's market capitalization

Market Capitalization   Share Price x No. of Outstanding Shares

Profit/CF Ratio =

Operating Cash Flow   Operation Cash

Flow

2.   Per-share basis

Price/CF Ratio =   Share Price Operating cash Flow Per
Share

GROWTH

Here is another key savvy step for the selection of winners. Does
your company expand? You want to know if your company is
growing or just depreciating in value. As an investor, you must
know how to choose carefully a firm that knows how to grow. Not
every firm or company are ready to widen their scope of income.
This is important because you will always be at the receiving end.
And stock with faster growth tends to command higher prices as
measured by such valuation ration as P/E.

Also, know the growth story of the company you want to invest
in. Consider the quarterly growth, check the trailing 12-month
growth, and then collect the data for calculating the four-year
annualized growth of your company. For a current update, check
the estimated current-year growth. What is the estimated next-
year growth? And you may want to know the estimated five-year
annualized growth to better project your future value to be
derived from such a firm.

PROFITABILITY

The third way to assess a stock is to check its profitability. To make an investment (buy or sell your decision), you must pay attention to and review the company based on its profitability. How well can the firm make the most of what they have? How resourceful is the company? How much of unnecessary expenses are they able to identify and divert to necessary areas of investment? Is it a firm that could get its expenditure straight? As an investor, you must know that the profit of stocks varies from industry to industry. Check profit margin (measure profit), returns on assets, and invested capital.

CHAPTER TWENTY

DIVERSIFICATION STRATEGIES

"Mutual funds have historically offered safety and diversification. And they spare you the responsibility of picking an individual stock."

Ron Chernow

Imagine an artist who wants to paint an already-drawn work. He stands set, looking at his sketches dangle across the canvas, his brush, varnishes, and various colors of paints fill his palettes. A bland sketch of a beautiful panorama which he captured on his last vacation in Canada, lay boringly on the canvas. He needs to add some color.

Suppose he paints the entire drawing in blue, probably because blue paint cost lesser than others, what would you think? Someone might walk in and view his work as a summer sky, while another person might perceive it as a deep blue sea. But what the artist had in mind is something entirely different, and he would have to show people what he expects them to see by only diversifying the colors. Turquoise lake, green vegetation, rock-brown rocky mountains, and bright blue skies – Lake Louise, Alberta, Canada.

Very much like the artist considers a choice of painting his sketches in a monotonous color or a perfectly-blend mix of colors; investors have options on what to invest in the stock market. Just like the artist had to protect what he conceives in his mind by adequately rendering his sketches in different shades of colors, to avoid a loss of its beauty and fragrance. An investor has to make an option to protect their portfolio from a catastrophic loss.

The diversification strategy involves strategies for adding new products in new markets. Investors with diversified portfolios often bloom while others are looking for the next available cheaper paint. You can follow these strategies to diversify your portfolio.

Use multiple stocks: A range between 25-35 stocks gives a perfect blend of risk and return. Buy multiple stocks, not fewer than 25, and

certainly not more than 35. A lot of investors purchase become stock collectors – they buy stocks when they find one which they like and also buy when they have the money, holding them for years as they generate index funds in the long run.

Many investors do not consistently maintain a portfolio of 25 to 35 for two main reasons. Firstly, they claim that they do not have enough capital to purchase lots of stock. Usually, they fail to realize that not having enough funds is not a problem. With discount brokers, investors can purchase stock in bites rather than in shares lots. For instance, buy $1000 bites, rather than 100-share lots. Even if you have $1000 to invest, you can diversify. Invest the money in stock, and when you've set aside another $1000, buy a second stock and not more shares of the previous one.

Secondly, investors doubt that they can monitor the news involving 25 stocks, talk more of 35. The truth is, it's hard. But it's possible for a careful investor. A benefit of diversification is possible when you do not limit your portfolio size.

Purchase different types of stocks: You can buy different stocks from diverse markets:

Financials

Consumer discretionary Telecommunication services Utilities

Consumer staples Health care Industries Materials Technology Energy

Every investor doesn't need to own stocks from all ten sectors. But you have not diversified enough if your portfolio fails to feature stocks that include six of the sectors. You should also vary your stocks by size. Larger-caps are always safer, and smaller-caps offer

more significant growth. You can also diversify with foreign stocks and remember you may experience more trouble following up foreign news feed – and investing holds a lot of surprises, both on the downside and upside.

The brain behind Companies' Diversification

Individual investors are not, anyway, exclusive to diversify, companies diversify too. Diversification is a business growth strategy that is used by a company to develop new markets and expand markets they have not explored yet. To achieve this, companies add new products and services that will entreat the customers in this new market. Due to the opportunity diversity avails companies to spread through new markets, they can explore new avenues, and thereby make more profits.

Companies Diversify to Attain More Profits

Such a cliché, "One tree does not make a forest," becomes relevant here. A lone company may not make greater profits as would if joined together with other individual businesses. Although diversification can increase the cost of management and organizational inefficiency, to the extent that the portfolio as a whole is less successful than the individual companies, your company goals should be the opposite – companies that create higher profits when joined than they did as individual businesses. A diversified group of companies can enjoy greater flexibility and more options as the economy changes. Your company can employ the following steps in achieving your goal.

- Define your classification strategy.

- Draw up a list of your company's core.

- Look for an industry to diversify into that are growing or having the potential to grow faster than your current industry.

- List your options.

- Make strategic analysis to choose the best option.

There is a reduction in when Diversification is adopted

Diversification is a useful technique that reduces risk by distributing investments among various financial instruments, industries, and other categories. Companies make the option of diversifying to lessen the burden of bearing business risk as they share with other businesses. Thus, a risk reduction may maximize returns. But by investing in various sectors that would react in a different way to the same event, returns maximizes. Plenty of investment experts agree that diversification may not prevent a loss; it serves as an essential component of attaining long-range financial goals while minimizing risk.

Company Diversification Boosts Brand Image

It is as expected that large and diversified companies serve large clients, while small companies serve small clients. Diversification grants the opportunity to more variety and options for more products and services. If rightly done, it provides a tremendous boost to brand image and profitability. For example, adding toothbrushes to toothpaste, powder, or mouthwash under the same or different brand aimed at different segments is one way of diversifying.

Diversified Companies Defend and not Compete

Having only a business unit that may compete, diversified companies rather synergize than compete. Unless in cooperate strategy places primary attention on nurturing the success of each unit, the strategy will fail no matter how highly constructed. A successful corporate strategy must mature from and reinforce competitive strategy.

Types of Diversification Strategy

Also, Diversification requires that a company procures new skills and knowledge in product development as well as new insights into how the market behaves at the same time. More than that, a company needs also acquire new resources, including new facilities and technology, which increases the level of risk exposure of the government.

Concentric diversification Vertical diversification Horizontal diversification Conglomerate diversification

Concentric Diversification

Technology remains the same, while its marketing plan changes notably. The concentric diversification identifies that similarities exist between the industries in terms of technological position. It is through this strategy that the firm measures and apply its technological ability to an advantage. This it does through a conscientious change or alteration in the market strategy performed by the business. By doing this, the market value of a product is likely to rise and therefore gain higher profit.

Vertical Diversification

Ideally, diversifying clears market of inherent risk in any one investment while increasing the possibility of making a profit, or at least avoiding a loss. Vertical diversification deals with investing in very different securities, for example, you may choose to invest in securities traded in separate countries, or both clothing and pastry companies. Diversification may be as broad (investing in a wide range of stock market) or as narrow (investing in one or two securities) the investor chooses.

Horizontal Diversification

Such technology used here is quite far from the existing businesses. As it may be, the new products are not relating to the existing one, but somehow, loyal customers still patronize the products. Horizontal diversification tackles products and services that are not, in a sense, technologically relating, but still sustain the interest of current customers. This type of diversification is effective if the clientele is loyal to the old products, and the new product is of fair price and well promoted. Since the new products will get advertised with the same strategy as the old, it increases its dependence on the old one and hence, may cause instability.

Conglomerate/Lateral Diversification

This type of diversification is similar to horizontal, except that it focuses and targets new customers instead of existing ones. Usually, the company promotes products and services without a commercial or technological relation to the old products and services. However, some existing customers might still retain an interest in the new products. This diversification is unique to the current business and can prove risky or simultaneously, more successful since it self- sufficiently aims to achieve an improvement in the company's profit. Often, the high growth scope promised, and the high return on investment in a new market segment may lead a company to take this option.

Diversify. Yes or No?

Although Mark Cuban, American entrepreneur and investor, in an interview, said, "Diversification is for idiots," you may also need to consider the view of another American options trader.

"If you invest and don't diversify, you're literally throwing out your money. People don't realize that diversification is beneficial even if it reduces your return. Why? Because it reduces your risk even more. Therefore, if you diversify and then use margin to increase your leverage to a risk level equivalent to that of a non-diversified position, your return will probably be greater."

Jeff Yess.

For decision making purposes, I will list some advantages and disadvantages of diversifying your stock market.

Disadvantages

Entities who are wholly involved in profit-making sections will enjoy profit maximization in financial management. However, a diversified entity that picks up the "expert" advice of limiting investment in the specific section may lose out. Therefore, diversification limits the growth opportunities for an entity.

New skillsets are necessary for diversifying, and this may be difficult for an investor to manage. Monitoring feeds and following up on the different stocks might prove challenging for the investor. Also, employing different strategies for diversifying which the investor might not be familiar with may appear tasking.

A poorly managed diversification or excessive ambition can lead a company into overly expanding into too many new directions at the same time. Consequently, all previously existing sectors of the investor will suffer a lack of attention with barely any resource that suffices.

The more the investor has at hand, the less their ability to individually focus on each. A widely diversified company might not quickly respond to market changes. Focus on operation will be limited, thereby making innovation scarce within the entity.

Advantages

The state of the economy is a significant factor dictating cash flow. As the economy changes, the spending pattern of people changes – whether higher or lower. A fabulous benefit of diversifying into several companies or product lines is that it helps to build a suitable balance for the investor during economic joggles.

An investor cannot calculate the risk involved in an investment; unpleasant surprises arise. A benefit of diversification is granting the investor willing shoulders capable of bearing the burden of a loss.

Diversification provides an opportunity for small investors. Most times, a platform for the use of potentially underutilized resources becomes maximized when diversified. For instance, a mouth-washing agent company may diversify with a toothbrush company, thus becomes identified with the latter company, and can ride as long as the toothbrush company does.

Finally, certain industries may collapse for a specific time frame owing to economic factors. But, when diversifying with a few other companies, its sustenance is maintained in the long run. When returns fall for a particular product, a diversified investor is hopeful of getting returns on other investments. Instead of falling flat on the back, such an investor is collectively picked up again by the profits they garner from other products. Diversification offers a backward movement from activities that may be declining.

CHAPTER TWENTY-ONE

HOW TO CREATE A SUSTAINABLE PORTFOLIO

"The stock market is filled with individuals who know the price of everything, but the value of nothing." –

Phillip Fisher

Creating a portfolio in stock marketing involves the activities of classifying financial assets, which include bonds, stocks, cash counterparts, and currencies and also their funds' equivalents, which include exchange-traded, mutual, and closed funds. Securities that are non-publicly tradable can also make up a portfolio such as private investments, real estate, and investments. Accounts like the Money market makes proper use of this notion to function adequately.

A great investment in knowledge in this aspect of stock investing would definitely pay off!

"An investment in knowledge pays the best interest" – Benjamin Franklin

How is a portfolio managed?

Conventionally, a portfolio is directly held by investors and is managed by money managers and financial experts. A good investor would build an investment portfolio according to the objectives of the investment and the 'risk tolerance.' Depending on the objectives of an investor, there could be various portfolios to suit different purposes.

Steps to building a sustainable portfolio:

In the marketplace of finance today, a well-sustained portfolio is pertinent to the success of any investor. It is needful as an investor or an individual to be well knowledgeable on how to determine an allocation of assets that best suits his or her goals and risk tolerance of your personal investment. Therefore, your portfolio as an investor or individual should meet the future capital requirements and also put you at rest. The following are approaches to constructing portfolios that are in unison with strategies of your investments.

Step one: Determine your appropriate asset allocation

The first assignment in the creation of a sustainable portfolio is determining your financial situation and goals as an individual. Pertinent items to put into consideration are age, time available for the growth of your investment, and also the capital for investing the future, and income needs.

Another factor to put in mind is your individual personality and risk tolerance. Are you capable of bearing the loss of some money for the expectation of greater returns? It is not needful if this will derail your peace of mind. However, there are chances that the high returns from these asset kinds are not worth losing your peace of mind over.

In understanding your present circumstances, your needs for capital, the future, and your risk tolerance will predict the allocation of your investments among the varying asset categories. For the possibility of a greater return, there would also be a possibility of a greater risk loss; this is termed as a principle of 'risk/return tradeoff. As an individual, you would not want to do away with risks because they can be optimized for your lifestyle and situation as an individual.

For instance, a young person who would not be needing his or her investments as a source of income has the ability to take greater risks when compared to an older person who is close to retiring. His or her goal would be to secure his or her assets and pulling income from them in a manner termed 'tax-efficient.'

"in investing, what is comfortable is rarely profitable" – Robert Arnott

At times, stepping out of your comfort zone will help you realize massive profits. There are aggressive and conservative investors. What does this mean? Basically, the greater the risk one can take, the more aggressive one's portfolio becomes, thereby allocating much more portion to equities and a lesser amount of bonds and the other fixed-income securities. Likewise, the greater risk you can bear, the more conservative your portfolio. The target of a conservative portfolio is to secure its value.

Step Two: Achievement of the Portfolio

After making up your mind on the allocation of the right asset, you are then to put a division of your capital among the suitable asset classes. Basically, this does not pose difficulties, as bonds and equities are equities. Moreover, you can divide the different asset classes into sub-classes, which also possess different risks and expected/potentials returns. For instance, as an individual or investor, you might make up your mind to split your portfolio's equity amongst various industrial sectors and between foreign and domestic stocks and companies that possess different market capitalizations. The portion of the bond that has the probability of being allocated among those that are long and short-term, corporate versus government debt, etc.

There are varying ways one can go about selecting assets and securities to achieve your asset allocation strategy. It is also important to take note that as an investor analyzing the potential and quality of every asset you invest in is needed. How is this achieved?

Stock Picking

Select stocks that match the risk level you have in mind to carry in the equity portion of your portfolio; sector, stock type, market cap are factors to put into consideration. Do an analysis of the companies that are making use of 'stock screeners' to narrow down potential picks and then embark on a deeper analysis of each potential purchase in other to control the risks and opportunities. This then is the most work-intensive medium of including securities to your portfolio and needs you to consistently put an eye on the changes in price in your holding and keep tabs on new information or changes on industry news and company.

Bond Picking

In the process of bond selection, there are different factors to bear in mind. Each includes the bond type and coupon, maturity, credit rating, and the interest rate of the environment in general.

Mutual Funds

This kind of fund is existent for a large range of asset classes and enables an investor to hold his or her stocks and bonds, which have been picked and researched by experienced fund managers. Definitely, when the fund managers are paid for their services, it will tell on your returns. Index funds have created another way out; they have lesser fees due to the fact that they picture an index that is already established and is then properly managed.

Exchange-Traded Funds (ETFs)

This fund can serve as an alternative choice if you decide not to put your investments in mutual funds. This fund system is mutual funds that operate their trading like stocks; its assets are offered in wide classes and is very handy when you are rounding out your portfolio. They are quite alike when compared to mutual funds in the sense that they are a representative of a large bucket of stocks normally classified by sector (capitalization), country, and others. However, they are different because they are not consistently managed. As a result of the passiveness in its management, its offer costs savings more than mutual funds while it supplies dynamism.

☐   Step Three: Reassessment of your portfolio weightings

"The individual investor should act consistently as an investor and not as a speculator." – Ben Graham.

After laying a solid foundation for your portfolio, you have a duty of ensuring its stability and doing a consistent analysis every period. This is because there is usually a change in the movements of price, and this might, in turn, bring a change to your initial weightings. In order to work out the actual asset allocation of your portfolio, quantitatively classify the investments and calculate the proportion of their values to the whole.

Other factors that have a potential of altering over time include your; risk tolerance, financial situation, and needs in the future. If there are changes, there might be a need for you to make adjustments to your portfolio accordingly. However, if there is a reduction in your risk tolerance, you should reduce the figure of held risk equities. In case you want to embark on greater risk and the allocation of your asset demands that a little proportion of your assets be held in more unpredictable small-cap stocks.

To bring re-stabilization, realize which of your positions are either overweighed or otherwise. For instance, if you hold 40% of your current asset in small-cap quantities, while your asset allocation, in

turn, should have only 20% of your assets in that class. Re-stabilizing or rebalancing has to do with the determination of the level of this position needed by you to bring to reduction and give allocation to other classes.

☐   Step Four: Strategically Rebalancing

After determining which of the securities you are to use, there is a need to bring in a reduction and by how much, make a decision on which of the underweighted securities you will be purchasing and also alongside the proceeds from the sales of securities that are overweighed. You can make use of the approaches discussed in step two in the selection of your securities. It is advisable to note that when you are in the process of rebalancing and bringing readjustments to your portfolio, do not forget to put into consideration the tax consequences of the sales of assets at a particular point in time.

Probably the growth stocks of your investment have greatly appreciated in times past, but then, if you have to sell off your equity positions in order to bring balance to your portfolio, you may incur important capital gains taxes. In cases like this, it might be of much more benefit to desist from contributing new funds to that future asset class while you keep on contributing to other asset classes. This will bring about a reduction in growth stocks' weighting in your portfolio in times past without the incurring of capital gain taxes.

Simultaneously, put the outlook of your securities into consideration. If you notice that the same stocks that have overweighed growth are threateningly going to fall, it is advisable to sell them irrespective of the tax consequences. You can put into use the opinions of analysts and reports from researches. They will help in gauging the outlook of your holdings. Tax-loss sales are also a selling strategy that can be applied for the reduction of the implications of tax.

During the whole period and process of the construction of your portfolio, it is important to bear in mind above everything that the maintenance of your diversification is a priority. Owning securities

from each asset class is not a guarantee; a diversification within each asset class is also needed. Put your holdings in place by ensuring that they are spread throughout a wide range of industry sectors and subclasses within a given asset.

Creating a sustainable portfolio depends on the aforementioned steps. However, one important point to be stressed on would be this question; 'How much risk can you handle' the level of risk you can handle would determine the extent of the sustainability of your portfolio.

"An investor who cannot master their emotions are ill-suited to profit from the investment process" – Benjamin Graham.

An investor who is ready to create a sustainable investment has to carefully sit and do an analysis of how much he or she can invest without it necessarily affecting his or her daily living, when he or she would need the money, how much he or she can invest, etc. factors such as your level of wealth, expectations, affect your risk tolerance. So, it is advisable that you carefully and properly draft out your income plan, expected income, and how much you intend to invest. These would help you in reaching your goal. Before proceeding to the final step of making the decision, you should consider the following things to avoid;

Forgetting inflation: It is important to ensure that the estimates of your spending reflect inflation.

Do not underestimate your needs and span of life: if you feel you would be living 15 years after you have retired, make plans for 20 years, and if you also feel you would need a $50,000-dollar year plan, it is advisable that you add $10,000 extra, making it $60,000. The point here is that; the greater the conservation of your estimates, the greater the possibility of achieving your investment goals.

Expectations that are not needed: For instance, if your needed rate is more than 10%, replace your assumptions. Let your

expectations and plans be visible and realistic.

CHAPTER TWENTY-TWO

NEXT LEVEL FOR BEGINNERS IN OPTION TRADING

Approval of option rates is a widely ignored field in options trading. When an individual opens an account, the broker assigns them one of several rates of option approval supposedly based on the expertise and needs of the option trader. Therefore, we will be considering this next level for beginners who are set to go into stock market investing.

Options Trading Levels

Level One:

An option trader is allowed to make covered calls at the first option acceptance point, as well as "long defensive puts." Now there is a catch; at this point, an investor is not permitted to buy any calls but is allowed to buy puts only in the amounts he or she keeps and also only in the same stock he or she owns.

For example, if a trader owns 100 stock shares, then they might buy a single put option, and nothing more. By the way, this is usually the only amount for IRAs (individual retirement accounts) accepted by most brokerages.

Level Two:

The level 2 approval option reflects an incremental change over the previous stage. At this point, it is acceptable for a trader to execute all Point 1 listed strategies and to go on long calls and puts.

At this point, you can buy a call directly or place on either optional stocks, exchange-traded funds (ETFs), or even indices.

The approval level is synonymous with the word speculation, at least from the point of view of the broker.

Level Three:

Level 3 choice approvals require spreads no matter whether they are lateral, horizontal, or vertical.

The same is not said for being long or short on a spread, though. When one is shortening a horizontal spread in an owned account without adequate funds, the broker will immediately deny the order.

Yet again, there is a cap on each of these various rates of approval for options. The next stage is the shortening of something without ownership.

Level Four:

Rate 4 of option acceptance is known as an exposed sale or naked shorting. (I prefer using the word "exposed" instead of "naked,"

particularly when I'm thinking about spread trading involving several positions, also known as legs. Sometimes, one of the positions could be revealed or exposed, so if I claim I've got a "naked leg," it sounds odd.) Level 4 is the highest level of approval, and just about any option strategy could be performed at this level as long as it's possible to execute.

Short selling is possible at this stage, as are several different forms of spreading ratios.

Key Steps for Next Level Option Trading

The goal of all traders is undoubtedly to make maximum profit with minimum investment and minimum risk. There are assets out there in the stock sector, which can meet the needs of any trader. But it is left to any trader to know how to make use of these. Every trader works differently, and so for some others, what looks good will not be the same. This is the very reason why buyers and sellers at any given time have the same assets.

When one thinks the market price is going to shoot up, another would have some other information to make them think the price is going to fall.

The seven important guiding steps in any binary options trader's life are:

1.   Knowledge of how to interpret charts

The use of binary option trading software would make huge profits for traders. One of the most important methods is to trading maps. When the trader puts effort into learning how each of these trading methods works, the anticipated benefits would be high.

It's true that in the trading platforms, almost all traders have these resources readily accessible, but not everyone knows how to view and use the same to make big money. The trader will be wise enough even before a trading indicator is loaded to guess how the markets are going and which strategy to use. This pace and care will certainly help traders on their path to success.

2.   Using tested trading strategies:

Using multiple tactics is popular but considers checking this before using it on the live market. Unless the techniques are put into action, the pros and cons will be hard to interpret. This is exactly the support that comes into play from demo accounts. Have a dry run of the binary options trading strategy before applying it to live trades using these demo accounts. Seek also to do these checks a bit ahead of trading live on the market. As the strategies which once worked well do not suit the current market conditions the same way.

3.   Making use of indicators:

Just because measures are delivered through a trustworthy network, it will result in failure to use them without consideration. Coping with the loss that is generated because of bad indicators would be difficult. Therefore, to prevent such scenarios- test the indicators and evaluate them before applying.

Using the trading indicators that are offered is good but being too dependent on them can affect long-term trading. Such sources of measures are not accurate for any investment loss. Therefore, it is worth spending your time evaluating it before doing business.

4.   Knowing why to avoid emotions while trading:

By now, you can be aware that trading is not an emotional game but logic and statistics. Such awareness will help you prevent suffering, which is at the expense of moral convictions and intestinal feelings. When you sell feelings, you'll soon see the negative effects. Repeated adverse effects on your investment will automatically cause you to take action, but in most situations, the loss of investments will be too large by the time this is triggered. Make a rational decision on powerful trade to regulate emotional measures.

5.   Adhere to the signals:

Traders will spend enough time to understand their power and weakness. By this, we mean it would be easy for traders to match their trading strategies according to their strengths as well as to focus on avoiding investing in weak points that they are not well-versed in. Seek to stop trading if the market conditions are not favorable and take advantage of this time when the market is up and healthy. Signals are just the signs that you need to take action, and no duty remains. This is done at the trade discretion.

6.   Trading based on the strengths:

In any strong binary options trader, being able to ascertain weakness and strength is the best quality to be seen. If your strength is to transact long-term trades, you should prepare the trading strategy accordingly, thus reducing the risk factor to a certain level. If this is an opportunity to avoid/reduce risk, it should be considered before any trading strategy is

finalized. Be frank with yourself, and be prepared to accept mistakes too. Also, when these characteristics are seen in traders, can they resolve the negative?

7.   Executing long term trades:

Binary options are not a perfect form of trading that you can immediately make money from. There are, of course, trader tales that have made money in a short time. But this is not a common trading feature of binary options. Be prepared to invest for the long term, say you can have noticeable growth in investment in a year's time. So, to invest in binary options for the long term, you should be cautious in achieving returns for the fund. Be rational about your goals, and remain committed to the trading strategies as well. It is important to understand yourself and the needs of binary option trading. This understanding helps you cross the difference between outcomes and expectations.

Having said these, it is now up to you to determine when to invest, how to invest, and which asset to select. Any benefit or loss is to be solitary to the dealer. Be sure to read about binary options trading sometimes on a regular basis, and what's new. This knowledge would be the main reason why others are through when you are still struggling in the same market conditions.

Although making money through binary option trading isn't very hard, unless you know exactly how it works, the returns will be exceptional.

How Tools can take your Trading to the Next Level Tools for Trading to a New Level

When an ordinary person first enters the stock market, they face a whole world; they know nothing about it. Specific technical principles, highly analytical market research strategies and asset-rate forecasting techniques, and psychological considerations are just some of the initial obstacles newcomers face! The time comes quickly when all of the experience and practice starts to pay off, and new online traders begin to search for strategies and methods to improve their business returns and trade more effectively. Today we're going to set out a range of resources that can take your trade to the next level. We hope this knowledge will be in use for beginners and experienced professionals alike.

So, to begin with, the approaches to increase productive trading can be divided into classes. Trading professionals currently separate instruments to improve productive trade into the following categories:

- Technical

- Psychological

Without a doubt, there are several subgroups in every category of resources to improve successful trading. We'll cover the most common ones.

Technical approaches for increasing trading effectiveness

The first thing a trader has to do is be vigilant when selecting a site to perform financial operations. Only technologically advanced, user- oriented, and efficient terminals provide the best prospects for a stable income generation. At this point, what tools you trade with is not relevant at all, be it SFD contracts, FOREX, short-term over-the- counter positions, or cryptocurrencies. To completely leverage the trade opportunities, all you need is a user-friendly interface and lucrative financial terms.

Here are several simple recommendations:

Be careful about how stable the platform is. It's an open secret that extracting income from the financial operations on the market is more straightforward than putting those profits into your bank account. Online trading is rife with conmen and fraud, so do your homework on trading sites, starting with what licenses they possess, first and foremost when selecting a partner. The vast majority of multinational companies today are no longer working in a legitimate gray zone. They have legal requirements and instruments for trading online.

Look how user-friendly this terminal is. The toolkit of the platform offers the conditions required for the traders to build different strategies. That is, the wider the range of resources the terminal has to offer, the greater the ability you need to develop a highly successful trading strategy.

Select a terminal that offers the best conditions for financial trading, depending on your needs. It's all pretty simple; identify your financial skills in advance and the total amount of funds you will gamble on the market. Then, use money management strategies to set yourself limits. Decide on a platform based on your criteria, which will establish the ideal conditions for market work.

Act jointly with helping clients. They can give lots of good advice and details. Currently, when a partner, meaning you, hemorrhages trading money, platforms are placed in a bad spot, as they work mostly off commission. That's why clients who extend a hand have started to attract skilled analysts who consult free traders. A firm help will carry the trade to a fantastic new standard in terms of results.

Of course, you need to provide approaches in terms of technological resources to improve successful trading. Such market evaluation mechanisms and the guidelines traders obey when dealing in detail are more critical tools to make a reliable profit. You will also have as broad a range of tactics in your arsenal as possible.

To have the most successful arsenal of trading systems that you can, you must research the different forms. Research should not constitute a problem; you can make research split in systems as:

- Technical analysis strategies and

- Fundamental analysis system

When you want to improve how efficiently you trade, then each community will follow some of its best strategies. Then, you can build contracts that deliver outcomes in all market conditions and use all financial assets and business resources for cryptocurrency. Finding methods to choose from isn't difficult; there is a broad range of methodological approaches available online. Here, too, we have easy recommendations:

Aim to put together your own trading plan, one that represents all of your personal interests on market trading, knowledge, and practices. Experience has revealed that the traders who achieve the best results use systems they have built themselves.

Not all successful approaches are that way at first glance. That is why you must still check all the approaches to trading yourself. And you can understand better how the programs work for you, with your own practical experience, without relying on a third party's advice.

Strategies aimed at unique conditions. There is no overarching policy on trade. So be prepared, as even the most successful program will bring losses in some circumstances!

Build your own portfolio of powerful trading structures. You will increase your market analysis capacity and thus improve the overall effectiveness of your trade.

Bill Williams' range of metrics, arguably one of the most talented analysts and traders, can be used as practical tools of research to evaluate how efficiently you sell. All in all, his analytical services allow you to achieve the best possible outcomes through clearly worked-out methods for their realistic market research application. A total of 6 predictor tools are available, which can be used as a basis for creating more efficient trading strategies. We recommend these predictive tools to improve the efficacy of your stock trading:

- AC (Accelerator/Decelerator)

- alligator indicator

- fractal indicator

- gator indicator

- MFI indicator

- awesome oscillator indicator

Thanks to simple market measurement algorithms, Bill Williams has been able to develop more powerful tools that can boost the trading performance of any trader. As you can see, the technological approaches to boost how efficiently you sell in terms of format are

relatively   easy. When you   do   apply these   guidelines   correctly, however, you will produce the full number of indicators.

Psychological Approaches to Improving Your Trading Results

Many beginners pay no attention to commercial psychological aspects. That is an utter error. Psychological factors play an important role in trading outcomes for an investor in the vast majority of cases. If they feel good or negative, either way, it is of no significance; traders will lose anything if they do not examine their own mental state. Psychology is also an important element of productive commerce.

The effect of the mental state of an investor on their trading, the overwhelming majority of financial market participants considers the fear of losing funds through trading as the leading factor which psychologically influences traders. Of course, the financial issue is significant, but in particular, these anxieties cause more problems than inexperience or a lack of specific skills. In this regard, it should be noted that traders who generate stable and reliable indicators while trading with minimal funds will see a decrease in their effectiveness while investing larger amounts in trading positions. That is motivated in particular by psychological factors. Investors are only afraid of wasting considerable resources and end up making several errors because of that.

The solution to these problems is straightforward and needs no input from specialists. It's easy; you can go back to a level of finance where you feel relaxed. Simply put, just trade in funds that you can risk without causing any problems. For each, the limit will be different. This will help you to learn the skills you need to train for when you're going up to a higher level. The sector, in general, divides traders into two fairly equal classes:

Investors who regulate their emotions while the trading-this category is usually more effective and generates the most indicators.

Traders who cannot manage their emotions in terms of trading –

These investors will sooner or later lose their money.

At any point, when trading, both groups aim for psychological perfection. Human beings are creatures that are so powerful. We have the power to attempt to solve almost every psychological problem, simply by evaluating the first time it emerged. Let's assume you are afraid of losing large sums of money as a simple example. The explanation for this is that without the requisite expertise and experience, you progressed to a higher level of trading that would ensure you were assured in yourself. The solution to this is simple. Use less money and get technical education. The gradual experience will offer trust and the requisite information to trade with a larger account.

Investors need to follow these basic rules to overcome psychological problems and emotional factors.

In any situation, remain cool. Market conditions are also difficult to deal with due to rapid swings in asset values, movements, or volatility spikes, which are difficult to forecast. This heightens the psychological burden on traders and leads to errors. Keep your emotions in check or set aside the emotional exchange. An alternative option is to commence low-cost contract trading.

Adhere strictly to the laws of your trading strategy. It's not worth changing your emotion-based trading system. Scientific research is not an objective study. In certain conditions, any strategy may fail. However, qualified plans take risk factors into account; the possible amount of loss shouldn't bring you to your knees, putting everything in jeopardy. Editing your program is almost always a mistake; just obey the strategic law and stick to your strategy.

The trading mechanism is regulated continuously. It's a very useful strategy to keep a trading journal where you're taking note of any trading position and the circumstances it has created. So, you can overcome both technological trade issues and psychological factors.

Don't mistake the choices the second time. Many traders are familiar with the situation where their strategy sends out a strong signal for placing a bid, but they are uncertain about the accuracy of the signal for one reason or another, or they want to wait for more suitable conditions to enter the market! The prices, however, leave the zone to place a contract, and the trader loses their chance to shape a lucrative trading spot! Many investors are facing this dilemma, so put your doubts aside and follow your trading plan and strategy when working on the market.

When you put the above psychological and technical trading conditions in place, you can eliminate almost all the emotional factors that affect trading. Regardless of the feelings or state of mind of an investor, you will become more focused on your plan, the most powerful method for generating income. Therefore, thanks to the precision of your technical trading approach, you can take it more effectively and not struggle in vain with your fears and anxieties.

CHAPTER TWENTY-THREE

FREQUENTLY ASKED QUESTIONS ON STOCK MARKET

"The stock market is filled with individuals who know the price of everything, but the value of nothing."

- **Phillip Fisher**

Are you lost, or confused about trading in a stock? Do you have some questions that have been bothering you? I do understand that you may be bothered about the numerous thoughts and questions popping up in your head, with nobody to ask. You are not alone on this; at every point in our lives, we learn something new, and despite the excitement that comes from learning, we may also be confused by a few things.

Having read through the previous chapters, it is expedient that you reflect on each chapter, beyond your launch out of your first stock market. However, you may encounter some challenges as you approach your first stock business, because of some questions you never got an answer to.

This chapter is focused on the frequently asked questions that newbies ask before launching into the market to purchase their stock. Each of these questions will help you expound on the chapter that has been discussed earlier, and also help you navigate through your thought.

What is a dividend?

I bet that this isn't the first time you are seeing or getting to know the word dividend, is it? A dividend is a commonly used word in the business/ finance industry; it is not only used in the stock exchange industry.

Whether you know the exact meaning of the word or not, the dividend is known as a portion or fragment of a company's profits that is paid to shareholders. In other words, the shareholders of

your company are the receivers of the dividend. Depending on the method of operation of the company or agreement they have with shareholders, the dividend is expected to be paid according to the shares of each shareholder, either as an extra incentive to motivate investors to buy stocks or on a quarterly basis.

What does this mean?

If Mr. Joe is a shareholder, who holds 20% of the total shares in mobile, and Telecommunications Company whose dividend is

500 million dollars, this means that the dividend that Mr. Joe receives from the company will be 100 million dollars.

However, some company does not pay their dividends to investors; this also depends on the structure and policy of the company—the reason for this is to allow the space for development, and growth.

1.   How to choose the right company to invest in

There are various companies that you can invest in. However, each company operates differently. If the policy or the agreement of the company favors you, you will benefit from the investment in the long run. Albeit, choosing the right company should be a priority for you as a beginner. To choose the right company, keep the following tips in mind:

-          Invest in stocks that provide you the opportunity to have a clear and in-depth knowledge of the business and structure model of the company. For instance, if you want to invest in Apple or Amazon, you need crystal-clear knowledge of how these two companies run.

-          Invest in companies with excellent structure, top-notch strategy, and model. Great recognized brands on Forbes today are all great, and competent companies with a unique structure.

-          Checkmate the financial health of the company. Do they have law cases in court? How many times have they run into

bankruptcy? How many recognized shareholders do they have? What is the stock market saying about them? Do they always make headlines on subject matters like fraud, bankruptcy, or illegal marketing?

Investigate their quarterly reports, annual reports, debt, and the long-term goals of the company. You can get every bit of information you desire on the internet or by asking people who have invested in the company previously.

For instance, you can ask your followers on Twitter to share their experience with a particular company that you wish to invest in. Their response will navigate your curiosity before you invest in the company.

-          Focus on companies that are willing to pay dividends to their investors. Like I mentioned earlier that each company has a policy that makes them different from others. Perhaps, a certain company has met the first three criteria that I have highlighted, but they do not pay a dividend to their investors. Would you rather invest in such a company?

Well, it is your choice to make. Albeit, it is more gainful to invest in a company that pays its dividends to an investor; at least it shows that you are enjoying the maximum benefit of your investment.

If you are still unclear about choosing the right company, I will recommend that you see a financial advisor to help you through this phase.

2.   What is the difference between forex trading and stock trading?

Forex market is different from the stock market, even though both are great means of investments. Just in case you do not know the difference between forex trading and stock trading, here is the main difference. When you trade forex, you are buying and selling currencies. It is different from buying stocks; when you are trading stocks, you are either buying or selling shares.

3.   What is the role of a shareholder?

I know you are excited about buying and selling shares, because of the profits. But, being a shareholder is far beyond just profits, there are responsibilities that you must take. The following are the responsibilities of a shareholder:

-        A shareholder brainstorms, and makes decisions in the company. A company's director has no right to make decisions, create a change, remove or replace a major manager, or executive in the company without informing the shareholders.

-        Shareholders decide how much the employees, staff, and directors of the company earn.

-        Shareholders have the power to make changes to the constitution, or policy in the company.

-        Shareholders make, check, and approve financial projects, and statements of a company.

4.   How can I become a stockbroker?

You definitely know by now that stocks are bought and sold; however, not everyone who buys and sells stocks is a stockbroker.

In the business world, there is always a middleman, which is most times a distributor. In the stock industry, a middleman is known as a stockbroker.

What is the duty of the stockbroker?

- A stockbroker can sell and buy stocks

- A stockbroker can become a consultant; they can offer advice to people who are interested in the stock market.

- A stockbroker may be employed to monitor the stocks of an investor.

Being a stockbroker can be very challenging, but it is lucrative, and you have to know your options if you must succeed. To become a certified broker, you need to be a registered member of the Financial Industry Regulatory Authority in your country and pass your exams.

5. What is the minimum amount to buy a stock?

This is a very common question that people ask. Well, you can invest any amount on shares. However, just people you start investing save at least your income for six months. So, if your income is $1000 per month, and you save $500 per month, at the end of 6 months, you would have $3000. That is enough to buy some shares and give you some mouthwatering profit.

6. What is the difference between mutual funds and stock exchange?

As I mentioned, there is numerous investment plans that can give you some good profits, but you need to know what is best for you. Mutual funds are different from the stock exchange, as a matter of fact, they do not share the same similarities, aside from the fact that they both yield profits.

The stock market involves the use of investing in the shares, and stocks of a company, to become a shareholder, and make profits. While mutual funds, on the other hand, is a collective investment that involves different kind of investors, to buy things like bonds, money, or stocks.

7.   What happens   when I   lose   my   moneyin
      the   stock market?

Every business has its own ups and downs and believe me when I tell you that the stock market is not any different. You may lose your money in the stock market for several reasons, including one of the most common reasons – the stock market crash.

A stock market crash is a sudden decline in the prices of stocks across the stock market. When this deflation happens, it leads to a significant reduction in paper wealth. When this happens, what should you do? Get yourself together, get some good counsel from financial advisors, heal from the loss, learn from the event, and invest again.

8.   What does it mean to short a stock?

Shorting a stock is the same thing as to the above heading, and it is the act of borrowing some stocks, according to your needs from stockbrokers, intending to sell them to other buyers who want. Albeit, shorting a stock does not occur every time; it often happens when the stock is believed to be overvalued. Due to the risk that accompanies this form of exchange, a broker, or a buyer may run into a great loss.

Shorting your stock is a highly risky and painstaking strategy; if it works, then you will have your gains and nothing to lose. If it fails, you will regret, and wish you never took that decision.

Also, it is necessary to verify rumors about the stock market before making a move with your stock. The truth remains that longing your stock is safer.

9.   How can I measure the health of a stock?

Like every disease in the world has its signs and symptoms; similarly, every stock has its signs and symptoms to show if it is healthy or unhealthy. Numerous indicators can predict the outcome of a stock, describe how healthy stock is. There are a few tips to help you recognize a healthy stock.

-            Carefully compare the ratio of the company's total earnings, divided by the total numbers of investors to have. The answer will reveal to you the earnings per share of the company.

-            Investigate the price-book ratio. The essence of the price- book ratio is to help you predict the value of the stocks; in comparison to the actual price, the shareholders are willing to buy them.

When the value of the stock is less than 1, it shows that the stock is trading less than its actual value. It also indicates that it is the best time to buy stocks, especially when the stocks are the same type.

-            Investigate the future of the stock market. The price of a stock per dollar will help you indicate the future movements of the market.

For example, when you find a stock with a lower price-earnings ratio, it could indicate that hard times, or the prices of the stock has increased. On the other hand, higher price-earnings could indicate a good time

Here are some frequently asked questions about the stock market. If you still have lots of questions on the stock market and stock exchange, I would recommend that you should ask your financial advisors some questions.

CONCLUSION

There is nothing worthwhile that doesn't require anyone to engage in specific values and timeless principles. Likewise, every organization, individual, and nation that are making a great mark in their field of expertise were all borne out of strictly followed morals, values, principles, and ethics.

I believe that by now, you've gotten hold of the facts that have been spelled out in this book. You should have understood how you could attain your financial destination without losing money.

As you continually lay hold of the concepts in this book, take advantage of expanding your knowledge about stock investing. Ensure you delve deeper into all that has been analyzed here.

Sometimes, trading can seem like taking a ride on a roller coaster. Sometimes, it can be an exciting and pleasant experience. At another time, you may become worried and afraid. Whatever happens neither panic nor give up.

A great trader is always dedicated to being the best at whatever he/she finds to do. Thus, the secret to a successful trade is to constantly have an un-quenching desire to expand your knowledge base.

Interestingly, it doesn't matter what your financial stand is, you can begin to work towards your goals for a wonderful future. Although the journey still continues, the strategies here will get you started. Whether you desire a healthy lifestyle, save enough for your retirement, provide a happy home for your family; you can increase your chances of attaining your goals by putting your money to work.